DK POCKET EYEWITNESS
SCIENCE

FACTS AT YOUR FINGERTIPS

Penguin
Random
House

DK DELHI
Project editor Rashmi Rajan
Project art editor Pankaj Bhatia
Senior editor Kingshuk Ghoshal
Senior art editor Rajnish Kashyap
Editor Surbhi N Kapoor
Jacket designer Juhi Sheth
Jackets editorial coordinator Priyanka Sharma
DTP designers Jaypal Singh,
Syed Md Farhan, Dheeraj Singh
Picture researcher Sakshi Saluja
Managing editor Alka Thakur Hazarika
Managing art editor Romi Chakraborty
CTS manager Balwant Singh
Production manager Pankaj Sharma

DK LONDON
Senior editor Fleur Star
Senior art editor Rachael Grady
Jacket designer Surabhi Wadhwa
Jacket editor Claire Gell
Jacket design development manager
Sophia MTT
Production editor Rebekah Parsons-King
Production controller Mary Slater

Publisher Andrew Macintyre
Associate publishing director Liz Wheeler
Art director Phil Ormerod
Publishing director Jonathan Metcalf

Consultant Penny Johnson

TALL TREE LTD
Editors Rob Colson, Joe Fullman, Jon Richards
Designer Ed Simkins

This edition published in 2018
First published in Great Britain in 2013 by
Dorling Kindersley Limited
80 Strand, London, WC2R 0RL

Copyright © 2013, 2018 Dorling Kindersley Limited
A Penguin Random House Company
10 9 8 7 6 5 4 3 2 1
001–310520–May/2018

A CIP catalogue record for this book
is available from the British Library.

ISBN: 978-0-2413-4369-2

Printed and bound in China

A WORLD OF IDEAS:
SEE ALL THERE IS TO KNOW

www.dk.com

CONTENTS

What is science?

Science is the study of the Universe and everything in it – from the tiny atoms that make up all matter to the forces that build stars and planets. Through the study of science, we have been able to work out how our planet came to exist, and how life on Earth developed. We are even able to work out how the Universe might come to an end in the far future.

Materials science

Science can be split into three main areas – materials, physical, and life science. Materials science looks at what materials are made of, how they react with each other, how they can be combined to form new materials, and what uses they can be put to. Chemists often carry out research to create useful things rather than simply to learn about the world.

Chemicals reacting in a flask

Physical science

Scientists who study forces, energy, and how they interact, try to answer some big questions. How was the Universe formed? What are the forces that hold it together? Where does energy come from? What is light made of?

Beam of white light

Light is split by a prism

Life science

Life scientists study all living things, such as bacteria, fungi, plants, and animals. They observe how organisms live, what they eat, how their bodies work, and how they work together to form different ecosystems.

The eating habits of animals, such as this kingfisher, are studied in life science

What is a scientist?

Scientists discover laws that explain the world around us. They do this by making observations and then coming up with predictions, or hypotheses, for how they think things work. They then test these hypotheses in experiments to see if they fit the evidence.

White light is split into different colours

This scientist is developing new forms of wheat to improve farmers' crops

Scientific advances

Some scientific breakthroughs have changed the course of history. Inventions such as the wheel, penicillin, and the World Wide Web have transformed people's lives, while the development of theories on the laws of motion and natural selection have helped build our understanding of the Universe.

Inventions and theories

An invention is something that humans have created, which did not exist before. But scientists do not just come up with new inventions, they also develop new ways of thinking about how the world works.

Invention of the wheel
Invented in Mesopotamia, the first wheels were used as potters wheels, and were later attached to vehicles for transport.

c.9000 BCE

c.3500 BCE

c.1200–1000 BCE

The Iron Age
A new method was discovered to extract iron from iron ore through smelting (heating with carbon). Iron tools were harder and sharper than the bronze and stone tools of previous ages.

Agriculture
The development of farming in Mesopotamia allowed people to settle in permanent communities for the first time. This led to the development of large towns, such as Babylon.

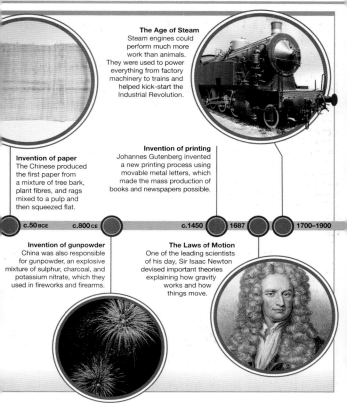

The Age of Steam
Steam engines could perform much more work than animals. They were used to power everything from factory machinery to trains and helped kick-start the Industrial Revolution.

Invention of printing
Johannes Gutenberg invented a new printing process using movable metal letters, which made the mass production of books and newspapers possible.

Invention of paper
The Chinese produced the first paper from a mixture of tree bark, plant fibres, and rags mixed to a pulp and then squeezed flat.

c.50 BCE   c.800 CE   c.1450   1687   1700–1900

Invention of gunpowder
China was also responsible for gunpowder, an explosive mixture of sulphur, charcoal, and potassium nitrate, which they used in fireworks and firearms.

The Laws of Motion
One of the leading scientists of his day, Sir Isaac Newton devised important theories explaining how gravity works and how things move.

Discovery of polonium and radium
The French-Polish physicist Marie Curie discovered the radioactive elements polonium and radium. Her work on radioactivity paved the way for a new understanding of atoms.

Albert Einstein
The theory of relativity (proposed in 1905 and completed in 1916) put forward by the physicist Albert Einstein fundamentally changed people's understanding of time, space, matter, and energy

Invention of cars
The invention of the petrol-powered automobile by Karl Benz at the end of the 19th century eventually brought the Age of Steam to an end.

| 1859 | 1885 | 1895 | 1898 | 1905–16 |

X-rays discovered
Wilhelm Röntgen discovered X-rays, which can be used to produce images of bones inside the body. This transformed medicine.

Natural selection
In his book *On the Origin of Species*, Charles Darwin put forward the revolutionary theory that species gradually evolve (see page 140) into new forms through "natural selection".

Penicillium
mould growing
in a Petri dish

Discovery of penicillin
Antibiotics have saved millions
of lives. The first antibiotic,
penicillin, was discovered by
accident by Alexander Fleming
when he noticed a strange mould
killing the bacteria in a Petri dish.

Invention of the World Wide Web
The British computer scientist Tim Berners
Lee linked up the world with his invention
of the World Wide Web, a global computer
communication system that uses the Internet.

1928   1958   1990

Invention of the microchip
The first computers were
big and slow. However,
Jack Kilby's invention of
the microchip (a set of
electronic components
etched on to a tiny
silicon chip) allowed
the development
of smaller, faster
computers.

Everyday science

Science does not take place just in laboratories. It forms part of almost everything we do, whether it is cooking food, playing with plastic toys, speaking to a friend on the telephone, surfing the Web, or travelling from one place to another.

Play

From plastic toys and computer games to the latest cutting-edge sporting equipment, science has nearly always been involved in developing and shaping the materials. Science is also used in the design of the equipment.

Work

Science is used in a range of jobs, helping to make them easier and more efficient. Machines can lift heavy objects, computers can process information and send messages, while the latest surgical equipment can help save lives.

Rest

Science even helps us to rest. In our homes, science is all around us. Thermostats control the temperature, ovens turn raw ingredients into tasty meals, while satellites in space beam radio, phone, and TV signals from all over the world into our homes.

SCIENCE IN SPACE
Space exploration is one of the greatest achievements of science. The International Space Station is a science laboratory in orbit around Earth, where astronauts carry out science experiments. Many new discoveries and inventions have been made during space exploration, including some that we use every day, such as water filters, adjustable smoke alarms, and scratch-resistant glasses.

Modern trainers use technology
that was first invented for

space suits

and moon boots

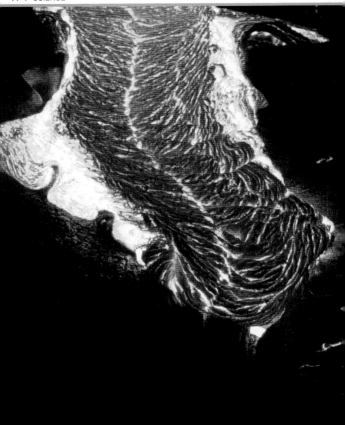

Matter and materials

Everything on Earth is made from different types of matter, which behave in different ways depending on the conditions. Rock, for example, can form solid mountains, but at high temperatures it melts and flows as lava. Exploring the way matter changes its form under different conditions of heat or pressure reveals how the Universe works at its most basic level. Understanding how materials behave in different situations shows how they can – and cannot – be used.

ATOMS
All matter is made up of tiny particles called atoms. At the centre of each atom is a nucleus, made up of protons and neutrons, and this is surrounded by a cloud of electrons.

States of matter

Matter is everywhere, but you cannot always see it. There are four main types, or states, of matter – solid, liquid, gas, and plasma. Each state is made up of moving particles, but they look and behave very differently.

Solids

In solids, the particles are packed together so tightly that they vibrate rather than move around. Solids can be hard or soft, huge or tiny, and everything in between, but they always have a fixed shape and volume, and occupy a definite space.

Particles are packed together in a solid

Liquids

The particles in a liquid are also close, but they are not held together as strongly as in a solid, so they can move around. This means a liquid has no fixed shape and usually takes on the shape of whatever container it is in. A liquid has a fixed volume, but it varies in thickness, or viscosity, which affects how freely it can flow.

Rocks and minerals are solids

Particles are close in a liquid

Honey has **high viscosity**, which means it flows slowly

Hot air, an example of a gas, expands to fill these hot-air balloons

Particles are spread apart in a gas

Gases

The particles in a gas are far apart and can move freely, so gases have no fixed shape or volume. Gases can be compressed (squeezed so the space between the particles decreases) or expanded (the space increases) to fit a container. Most gases are invisible.

Plasma

Plasma is rarely seen on Earth, but it is found throughout the Universe. Like a gas, it has no fixed shape or volume. However, it contains electrically charged particles (see pages 56–57) and exists only under certain conditions, such as in places with high temperatures or radiation. Streams of plasma can be seen in this plasma lamp.

Sulphur crystal embedded in rock

Changing states

A substance may not always remain in the same state of matter. It can change state when it is at different temperatures. For example, a solid can become a liquid if it becomes hot enough and a liquid may become a solid if it is cooled enough.

Boiling and evaporation

When water is heated to boiling point, bubbles appear. These bubbles are made because some of the liquid has changed to an invisible gas called water vapour, or steam. Water boils at 100°C (212°F). The water vapour escapes into the air in a process called evaporation. Evaporation can also occur more slowly. For example, wet hair dries because of evaporation.

Heat from within Earth causes the water to **evaporate**

Hot thermal spring in New Zealand

Condensation

The opposite of evaporation is condensation and this process occurs when a gas cools and becomes a liquid. When water vapour comes into contact with something cool, it turns back into a liquid. Condensation often forms on windows as the temperature drops overnight.

Freezing

When a liquid becomes cold enough, it will freeze and become a solid. The temperature at which a substance turns into a solid is called its freezing point. Water freezes at 0°C (32°F) and its solid state is called ice. Jet fuel freezes at around −47°C (−52°F).

Melting

When a solid is heated to a high enough temperature, it becomes a liquid, or melts. The increase in temperature causes the particles in the solid to move more freely until eventually they achieve a liquid state. The temperature at which a solid becomes a liquid is known as its melting point. The melting point and freezing point of a substance are the same temperature.

Solid ice lollies melt to form a liquid

The water cycle

Earth's water is constantly changing state as it circulates between the sea, the land, and the sky. This process is known as the water cycle. Although water is always moving, the total amount of water in the world always stays exactly the same.

Water and the atmosphere

The Sun's heat causes liquid water to evaporate, turning it into a gas called water vapour. As it rises in the sky, the vapour cools, condensing into tiny droplets, which gather together as clouds. Water falls back to the surface as rain or snow and eventually returns to the oceans – where the process begins again.

When water vapour cools high in the sky, it **condenses** and forms clouds

Condensation

Water heated by the Sun **evaporates**, forming water vapour

Evaporation

Small water droplets in clouds merge together to become larger ones, eventually falling to Earth as **precipitation**, such as rain and snow, when they become too big

Liquid water that has fallen as **rain** or melted from **snow** collects in rivers and streams

At low temperatures, water **freezes** into solid snow as it falls

Freezing

Precipitation

Melting

Over time, flowing groundwater can slowly wear away rocks, forming **underground caves** and **pools**

Some water sinks into Earth as **groundwater**, and eventually returns to the surface as springs or marshes

Properties of matter

Different substances have different properties. They might be hard or soft, flexible or rigid, flammable or not. Testing the properties of a particular substance helps in determining what it can, and cannot, be used for.

Mass and density

The amount of matter within an object is known as its mass. On Earth, the force of gravity (see page 84) pulls on the mass of an object to give it weight. An object's density is how much mass it has for its size. For example, a piece of iron weighs more than a feather of the same size as it is a denser material.

A feather has a low density

An iron bell has a high density

Plasticity

Some materials can be shaped into a different form. This property is known as plasticity. Modelling clay, for example, can be shaped into various objects. Special types of plasticity include malleability, where a material such as metal can be beaten into thin sheets, and ductility, which allows a material to be pulled into a thin wire.

Modelling clay has high plasticity, but the knife is less elastic and breaks easily

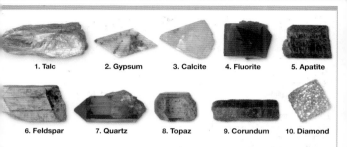

1. Talc 2. Gypsum 3. Calcite 4. Fluorite 5. Apatite

6. Feldspar 7. Quartz 8. Topaz 9. Corundum 10. Diamond

Hardness

The hardness of minerals is measured using the Mohs scale. Ranging from 1 (soft) to 10 (very hard), the scale measures how well one mineral can resist being scratched and shaped by another. A diamond could scratch any other mineral, but talc can easily be scratched by any mineral, or even a human fingernail.

Elasticity

Some materials are very flexible, and have the ability to bend. Some are so flexible that they can bend or stretch in different directions, but still return to their original shape, size, or position. This property is known as elasticity. A rubber band is an elastic object. Many materials cannot be stretched beyond a certain point, called the elastic limit.

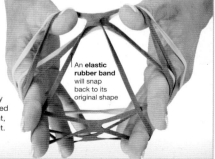

An **elastic rubber band** will snap back to its original shape

Flammability

If a material is flammable, it catches fire (ignites) easily and then burns (combusts). Highly flammable materials, such as petrol, can be dangerous, but also very useful. Flammable materials produce heat as they burn. A material that will not burn is known as nonflammable.

Solubility

If a material can dissolve in a liquid, it is known as soluble. The liquid into which the soluble material dissolves is a solvent. Water is often called the universal solvent because so many materials can dissolve in it. Soluble materials include solids, liquids, and gases.

Potassium permanganate is a solid compound that **dissolves** in water

Stone is **nonflammable** and does not catch fire

Conducting electricity

All metals are good electrical conductors, which means they allow electrical currents to pass through them easily. Copper is widely used in electrical wiring. Insulating materials, such as glass and plastic, are poor electrical conductors. They are used to prevent electricity from flowing where it is not needed, such as through our bodies.

A special nonflammable fabric called CarbonX does not burn even when heated to an incredible 3,000°C (5,500°F).

Wood is a **flammable** material and catches fire easily

Copper wires

Plastic insulator covers

Conducting heat

Metals conduct heat well and are known as thermal conductors. Other materials, such as glass and plastic, do not conduct heat easily. They are called thermal insulators and they are very useful as they prevent heat from escaping.

A metal pan conducts heat from the cooker to the food inside the pan

Atoms

Atoms are the tiny building blocks that make up everything in the Universe, including ourselves. They are far too small to be seen, even with the most powerful microscopes. Billions of them could fit on to the dot of this "i". Yet atoms are themselves made up of even tinier subatomic particles called protons, neutrons, and electrons.

Inside an atom

Atoms consist of three types of particle. At the centre is a nucleus made up of protons, which have a positive electric charge, and neutrons, which have no charge. This is orbited by some even smaller negatively charged particles called electrons, which spin around the nucleus at great speeds. These particles are so tiny that most of an atom is actually just empty space.

Neutrons inside the nucleus have no charge

A carbon atom has 6 neutrons, 6 protons, and 6 electrons

Negatively charged **electrons** move around the nucleus in paths called orbits

Helium nucleus

Magnesium nucleus

Different atoms

A helium atom has just 2 protons, 2 neutrons, and 2 electrons, while a magnesium atom has 12 of each. Sometimes atoms can lose or gain electrons to become a special type of atom called an ion. When an atom loses electrons, it becomes a positively charged ion. If it gains electrons, it becomes a negatively charged ion.

PARTICLE ACCELERATOR

Scientists can learn more about atoms by smashing subatomic particles into each other at high speeds and then studying the results. They do this using machines called particle accelerators, such as the Large Hadron Collider (below) at CERN in Switzerland.

Positively charged **protons** lie inside the nucleus

Scientists smash atoms
together at close to the

speed of light

to split them into smaller,
subatomic particles

PARTICLE TRACKS
Subatomic particles, such as electrons, are not usually visible. However, inside this special bubble chamber filled with liquid hydrogen, the electrons leave behind tracks as they move, creating intricate spiral patterns.

Molecules

Most atoms do not exist on their own, but bond with other atoms – either ones of their own type or of another element – to form molecules. Atoms join together by sharing their electrons, a process known as chemical bonding.

Simple molecules

The natural state of oxygen is nearly always as a molecule, not an atom. An oxygen molecule is made up of two oxygen atoms, chemically bonded together. The oxygen in the air consists of molecules, not single atoms.

Oxygen atom

**Model of
oxygen molecule**

Complex molecules

A sulphur molecule is made up of eight sulphur atoms bonded together in a ring. The structure of a molecule can be shown by a formula. For example, sulphur has the chemical symbol S and is made up of eight atoms, so its chemical formula is S_8.

**Model of
sulphur molecule**

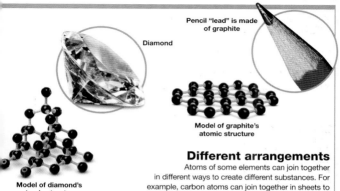

Pencil "lead" is made of graphite

Diamond

Model of graphite's atomic structure

Model of diamond's atomic structure

Different arrangements

Atoms of some elements can join together in different ways to create different substances. For example, carbon atoms can join together in sheets to form graphite or in a lattice shape to form diamond.

Complex chains

Some molecules are simple, containing just a few atoms. Others are very complex and may have hundreds or even thousands of atoms joined together in long chainlike structures, such as those in a vitamin A molecule.

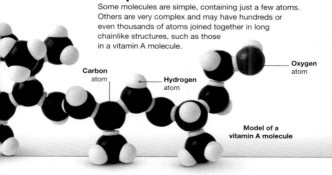

Carbon atom

Hydrogen atom

Oxygen atom

Model of a vitamin A molecule

Elements

A chemical that is made up of atoms of just one type is known as an element. Although all atoms are made of the same basic parts – protons, neutrons, and electrons – not all atoms are the same. It is the number of these parts that gives the atom – and the element – its properties.

Grouping elements

The number of protons in an atom of an element gives it its atomic number. Scientists arrange elements according to their atomic numbers in a chart known as the periodic table (see pages 144–45). Although each element is unique, many have similar properties. Those that share certain properties are grouped together.

Gold nugget

Au

GOLD

79

The atomic number of gold is 79

Alkali metals

The first group of similar elements in the periodic table is known as the alkali metals. These elements, which include sodium and lithium, are soft and react with water, forming alkaline solutions.

Sodium gets hot and melts when it reacts with water, producing hydrogen which burns

Transition metals

Most of the metals we use in everyday life, such as gold, iron, and copper, are grouped together as transition metals. This group contains metals that can create magnetic fields (see page 63) and are good conductors of heat and electricity.

The mask of the Egyptian pharaoh Tutankhamun is made of gold, a transition metal

Alkaline earth metals

Metals in this group, which includes barium, calcium, magnesium, and radium, are highly reactive, although not quite as reactive as alkali metals. Alkaline earth metals are found in numerous compounds in Earth's crust, as well as in our bodies. Bones contain calcium.

Limestone contains **calcium**, an alkaline earth metal

Limestone deposited by flowing spring water has formed terraces in Pamukkale, Turkey

Noble gases

The six noble gases – helium, neon, argon, krypton, xenon, and radon – are colourless, odourless, and usually do not react with other elements to form compounds. They are, however, used in a variety of applications including electric lights. Most noble gases glow brightly when electricity is passed through them. Lighter-than-air helium is also used in balloons and to lift airships.

The bright fluorescent colours of neon lights are caused by the glowing of neon and other noble gases

Poor and semi-metals

Poor metals have lower melting points than most transition metals. They are often used in alloys, such as bronze – a mixture of copper and tin. Semi-metals have some metallic and some non-metallic qualities. For instance, silicon is shiny like a metal, but brittle like a non-metal.

Tin, a poor metal, does not rust, and so it is often used as a coating for cans

Computer chips are made of silicon, a semi-metal

Non-metals

Non-metals are so called because they do not share physical or chemical properties with metals. Non-metals do not conduct heat or electricity well, and the solid forms of most non-metals are soft and brittle. The atmospheric gases nitrogen and oxygen are non-metals.

The striking surface of a matchbox is coated with phosphorus, a non-metal

Mixtures and compounds

Different elements can be combined to create new
substances. When atoms and molecules chemically
combine to form a substance, it is called a compound.
If no chemical reaction takes place – as when mud is
added to water – a mixture is formed.

**Two atoms of hydrogen and one
atom of oxygen combine to
form a molecule of water**

Compounds

These are often very different from the
elements that make them up. Hydrogen
and oxygen are invisible and odourless
gases. However, when chemically
combined, the two create a simple
compound called water.

**Water flowing at
Niagara Falls, Canada**

Mixtures

There are two main types
of mixture: solutions and
suspensions. In a solution,
a substance breaks up into
individual atoms or molecules
and mixes evenly in another
substance, known as the solvent.
In a suspension, a substance
does not break up completely,
and may still be floating in the
liquid as solid particles.

Ink will
mix evenly in
water to form
a solution

Mud **dissolves
unevenly** in water

Solution

Suspension

Alloys

Metals can be mixed with each other, or with other substances, to create a new substance called an alloy. Alloys have different properties to the substances they are composed of. For example, the alloy bronze is much harder than the metals that make it up – copper and tin.

Car wheels are often made of alloys

Separating mixtures

Several methods can be used to separate substances in a mixture, including evaporation, spinning, filtration, and distillation. The last method involves heating a mixture so that a substance with a lower boiling point can be collected as a gas from the mixture, leaving behind the substance (or substances) with the higher boiling point. Pure water can be obtained from salty water by distillation.

Oil refineries use distillation to separate petrol from crude oil

Reactions and changes

Physical changes occur when substances change state. Chemical reactions occur when the atoms in molecules are rearranged to create different molecules. Changes caused by physical reactions are usually easy to reverse, while chemical changes are not.

Chemical reactions

These reactions can be caused by various factors, such as heat or contact with other substances. When food is cooked, heat causes the ingredients to chemically react together, altering their appearance, temperature, texture, and taste.

Flour

Butter

Eggs

Sugar

Baking powder

Physical changes

Some changes are physical, not chemical. When candle wax is heated, it melts and changes to a liquid. However, its molecules do not change, just their physical state. The change can be reversed by re-moulding and cooling the candle wax.

Melting candle wax

Fast changes

Some changes can happen suddenly. When baking soda and vinegar are mixed, the two substances react, causing the liquid to erupt. The speed of change can also be altered: if a potato is cut into small pieces and heated in boiling water, it will change (soften) faster than if it were a single, large piece because the heat has less far to travel to get to the centre of the potato pieces.

The baked cake is chemically different from its ingredients

Baking soda mixes with vinegar to form a gas called carbon dioxide, causing the cork to pop

Slow changes

Certain reactions happen over a long period of time — days, weeks, or even years. Corrosion, such as rusting, occurs when metal objects are exposed for too long to the oxygen and moisture present in air, or other corrosive substances.

The car contains iron alloys that have corroded to form rust

A catalytic converter
from a car

Catalysts

Some substances, called catalysts, change
the rate at which a reaction occurs, although the
catalyst itself is not changed in the reaction.
Most cars are fitted with a catalytic converter,
which helps the polluting gases that fuel the car
to react and create less harmful gases. Many
catalysts speed up reactions, but others, called
inhibitors, slow down reactions. Preservatives,
added to food in order to keep it fresh for a
longer period, are examples of inhibitors.

Giving off heat

Some reactions release heat, light, or both.
These are called exothermic reactions and
include the burning of wood or other fuels
and reactions between acids and bases
(see pages 44–45), resulting in the formation
of a salt. The burning of fuel is also known
as a combustion reaction and can give off
enough energy to power a car or a house.

**The burning of a wick soaked in oil
gives out light and some heat**

Cool reactions

Endothermic reactions are the opposite of exothermic reactions. They absorb heat, rather than releasing it, to change the molecules. Special instant ice packs, used to treat sports injuries, contain water and ammonium chloride. When the pack is activated, the substances mix and react, causing an endothermic reaction which cools the affected area.

An ice pack being applied on the hand

Man-made materials

Sometimes chemical reactions are used to create substances that do not occur naturally. Man-made materials are often used for outdoor clothing. These breathable, waterproof materials are made when certain molecules are combined in a process known as polymerization.

Man-made waterproof clothing is popular with skiers and climbers

REACTIONS AT WORK
Firework displays are an example of exothermic reactions. They release heat and light. When a spark is applied, the fuse burns down, causing the gunpowder and metal stars within the firework to explode in a spectacular mix of bangs, crackles, and light.

The largest firework display ever, in Madeira, Portugal, in 2006 used

66,326

separate fireworks

Acids and bases

Acids and bases are chemical opposites: acids produce positively charged hydrogen ions and bases produce negatively charged hydroxide ions. Many acids and bases can be combined to produce useful substances, such as salts and soaps.

Acids

Some powerful acids are very corrosive, which means they can destroy, or "eat through", other substances. Weaker acids, such as lemon juice and vinegar, have a strong, sour taste. These are often used to flavour food, and can also be found in many household cleaning products.

Lemon contains citric acid

Seashells are made of a base called calcium carbonate

Bases and alkalis

Strong bases can be as dangerous as strong acids, although a base that destroys other substances is usually known as caustic rather than corrosive. Sodium hydroxide (caustic soda) can eat through some metals. Sodium bicarbonate, or baking soda, is a weak base, often used in cooking. Some bases are water-soluble and are called alkalis.

Detergent powder is formed by mixing acids and bases

Soaps

Mixing acids and bases

When certain acids and bases are mixed, they can react to produce water and a salt. Soap is made when a strong base is added to a fatty acid (a building block of fats found in our bodies and food), breaking it down to form a hard or soft soap (depending on the base).

Measuring acids and bases

The strength of acids and bases is measured using the pH (power of hydrogen) scale. It ranges from zero (strong acid) to 14 (strong base). Pure water is seven on the pH scale, which is neutral – neither acid nor base. The pH of a substance can be measured using a pH indicator such as litmus paper.

The colour of the indicator changes according to the pH of the substance.

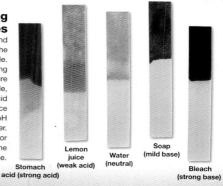

Stomach acid (strong acid)

Lemon juice (weak acid)

Water (neutral)

Soap (mild base)

Bleach (strong base)

Using materials

Throughout history, people have used and reused materials. Many natural substances can be adapted or changed to produce new substances. For example, soft clay can be turned into hard pottery, sand can be transformed into glass, and iron and carbon can be combined to form steel.

Glass

Glass is a mixture of substances, including silica (from sand), soda ash, and limestone. Glass can be formed into many different shapes. It can be blown into bottles and jars or rolled into flat sheets for windows. Other substances can be added to change the colour of the glass or to make it heatproof.

Molten glass can be blown or moulded into different shapes

Processing materials

Many materials can be processed to make different materials. For example, the raw material wood can be cut into building planks or broken into fibres and turned into paper. Paper itself can be torn into strips, mixed with glue, and used as papier-mâché.

Colourful papier-mâché figures on a carnival float

Recycling

Many objects and materials can be used more than once, even when they wear out. For example, tyres can be reused by adding new tread. Some objects can also be recycled – their materials turned into new objects. Aluminium cans, newspapers, glass bottles, and even electronic equipment are all regularly recycled.

Old computer circuit boards piled up in a recycling bin

Energy and forces

Everything in the Universe is constantly affected by energy and forces. A rollercoaster is a good example of energy and forces in action. Fuel provides the energy that is used to generate the force that pulls the coaster to the top of the slope. The stored potential energy the coaster has at the top is transferred to kinetic (movement) energy by the force of gravity as it runs downhill.

ELECTRICAL ENERGY
Computers use electrical energy to perform a range of tasks and to generate light. When you touch the screen of a tablet computer, you are applying a force to it.

What is energy?

Energy is what makes everything happen. It cannot be created or destroyed, but it can be transferred. For example, kicking a ball transfers energy from the person to the ball. Energy can also be converted from one form to another – as when the chemical energy in petrol is converted into the kinetic energy in a moving car.

Kinetic energy

The energy an object has because it is moving is called kinetic energy. A ball thrown into the air or a rollercoaster hurtling down a track both have kinetic energy. The greater the mass of an object and the faster it moves, the more kinetic energy it will have.

A ball flying through the air has kinetic energy

Chemical energy

Energy stored in substances is called chemical energy, and it can only be released through a chemical reaction. Chemical energy is stored in food, which must be broken down and its energy released by the body's metabolism.

Food stores chemical energy

Chemical energy stored in batteries is converted into electrical energy

Potential energy

An object can store energy and release it later. Stored energy is also called potential energy because it has the potential to make things happen. A coiled spring has potential energy, as does an archer's bow when it is drawn and ready to shoot an arrow. When the spring is not coiled and the bow not drawn, they have no potential energy.

Potential energy is stored in the string of the bow

Energy chain

Energy can take many different forms, from the heat of the Sun to the chemical energy stored in sugar. This energy chain shows how energy can be converted from one form to another.

Nuclear energy inside the Sun is converted into heat and light energy.

The green leaves of plants convert the **light energy** from the Sun into the **chemical energy** stored in sugar, by a process called photosynthesis (see page 115). Sugar is then stored in fruits.

Energy resources

Humans harness energy from many sources to supply power to their homes and vehicles. These include solar power, wind power, and nuclear power. The vast majority of our power, however, comes from fossil fuels, such as oil, coal, and gas.

Wind mills

When humans eat the fruits, the chemical energy is transferred to their bodies and used for all sorts of things. Winding up an alarm clock, for example, changes this chemical energy to **potential energy** in the spring of the alarm.

The potential energy of the wound-up spring is converted into the **kinetic energy** of the alarm bell and the **sound energy** of the alarm. The clock keeps working until the spring is unwound and has lost its potential energy.

Saving energy

One day the supply of fossil fuels will run out and we may face energy shortages. It is important to save energy, for example by using low-energy light bulbs and insulating homes. Many governments have also begun investing in reusable sources of energy, such as solar and wind power.

Solar panels absorb sunlight to produce electricity

Atom power

An enormous amount of energy is locked up inside the nucleus of an atom. This can be released by splitting the nucleus apart in a process known as fission. This energy can also be unleashed by fusion, which involves squeezing nuclei together.

Neutron

Unstable nucleus

Nucleus splits in two

Heat, light, and other forms of energy released

More neutrons released, hitting more nuclei

Nuclear fission

To release the power of the atom in a nuclear reaction, a neutron is fired at the nucleus of an unstable atom, such as uranium. This splits the nucleus, releasing energy and shooting out more neutrons. They then split other nuclei, releasing even more energy and triggering a chain reaction.

Using fission power

Fission reactions take place in a nuclear power station. Although only a small amount of fuel, usually uranium or plutonium, is used, huge amounts of energy are released. This superheats water, which is turned into high-pressure steam and drives the blades of a turbine. The spinning turbine drives a generator, which makes electricity.

Nuclear power station

Atomic explosion

Atomic bombs, or A-bombs, use nuclear fission to release massive amounts of energy with devastating effects. Hydrogen bombs, or H-bombs, use both nuclear fission and nuclear fusion to generate explosions that can be thousands of times more powerful than an atomic bomb explosion.

A test detonation of a US atomic bomb in 1957 throws up a giant mushroom cloud of debris

STAR POWER

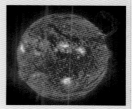

The Sun releases a lot of energy

Nuclear fusion releases energy by forcing nuclei together to form new elements. Fusion reactions are the source of the Sun's energy. Every second, deep inside its core, 635 million tonnes of hydrogen turn into helium.

Electricity

All atoms contain positively charged protons and negatively charged electrons. Electricity is a flow of charged electrons from one place to another. When electrons are transferred between substances, it can cause a build-up of negative charge in one place and positive charge in another – sometimes with powerful results.

Lightning

Inside storm clouds, tiny particles of ice rub against each other and electrons are transferred between particles. This leads to a build-up of negative charge at the bottom of the cloud. If this charge becomes large enough, it can jump between clouds or a cloud and the ground in a massive bolt of electricity, known as lightning.

A lightning bolt lights up the sky

Static electricity

When electrical charge builds up in one place it is called static electricity. If you rub your hair on a balloon, electrons are transferred from your hair to the balloon. This gives your hair a positive charge and the balloon a negative charge. Particles with opposite charge are attracted to each other, so your hair will stick to the balloon.

Hairs separate because particles with the same kind of charge repel each other

Current electricity

The electricity that powers our homes is known as current electricity. It flows from power stations to our homes and offices along long electric cables, which are made from conducting materials (see page 25). These cables are supported by structures called pylons, which are protected from the current by ceramic insulators.

Pylons support electric cables

Using electricity

The electricity we use around our homes and in our gadgets is produced in several ways. It can be generated in massive power stations located far away. On a smaller scale, gadgets such as torches and mobile phones can be powered by batteries, which provide electricity whenever we want.

Hydroelectric dam and reservoir

INSIDE A TURBINE

Electricity generator

Water from a reservoir flows down a chute

Turbine

When water is released from a hydroelectric power station's reservoir, it rushes past the turbine's blades, sending them spinning.

Generating electricity

Electricity is produced, or generated, at power stations. They use massive machines called generators, which contain large coils of wire that spin inside a magnetic field to produce electricity. The coils are connected to turbines – large wheels with blades that are pushed round by steam or water. The steam is produced by heating coal, oil, or gas, or using nuclear power. Water-powered turbines are found at hydroelectric power stations.

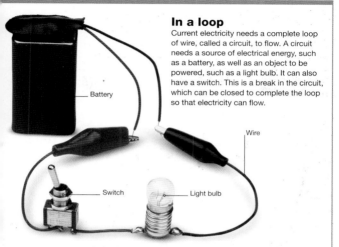

In a loop

Current electricity needs a complete loop of wire, called a circuit, to flow. A circuit needs a source of electrical energy, such as a battery, as well as an object to be powered, such as a light bulb. It can also have a switch. This is a break in the circuit, which can be closed to complete the loop so that electricity can flow.

Battery

Wire

Switch

Light bulb

A simple circuit

Storing electricity

Batteries store energy in chemicals. When a battery is put into a circuit it makes a current flow around the circuit. Batteries are very useful for small electrical devices that do not need much power, or for devices that need to be portable.

From 1950 to 2011,
the population of the
USA doubled, but electricity
use increased to more than

13 times

the amount used in 1950

BRIGHT LIGHTS
Twinkling lights show where the towns and cities are on this satellite image of the USA at night. The country generates more electricity than any other – more than twice the generating capacity of the second largest producer of electricity, China.

Magnetism

Magnetism is a force that can attract (pull towards) or repel (push away). Materials that are strongly attracted to magnets, such as iron or nickel, are called ferromagnetic materials. Some magnets are permanently charged with magnetism, while others are only magnetic when they are inside a coil of wire with an electrical current flowing in it.

Repel or attract

A magnet has two ends, or poles – a north pole and a south pole. When two magnets are placed near each other with like (the same) poles facing, the two poles will push each other away. If a north pole is facing a south pole, they will pull towards each other.

Iron filings show the direction of the magnetic force

S N   N S

Like poles repel each other

S N   S N

Opposite poles attract each other

Iron filings cluster near the poles where the magnetic field is strongest

North pole of magnet

Magnetic field

The area around a magnet where a magnetic force can be detected is called its magnetic field. The magnetic field is strongest near the poles. Dropping iron filings around a magnet reveals the shape of its magnetic field. The stronger the magnet, the larger its magnetic field will be.

Compass needles align with the **magnetic field**

South pole of magnet

Iron filings show **lines of force** around the magnet

Magnets in action

We use magnets in many different ways. The motors inside many machines are driven by small magnets, while large magnets can power trains. Compasses use Earth's magnetism to show us the way.

Electric motors

This toy car is powered by an electric motor, which uses magnets to produce a spinning motion. Electric motors are found in many machines. Washing machines and vacuum cleaners contain large motors, while the hands of a wristwatch are moved by tiny motors just a few millimetres wide.

Magnetic trains

A maglev train is moved by magnetism. Magnets under the train and on the track make the train hover up to 10 mm (0.4 in) above the track. The train does not have an engine, but is pushed forwards by another set of magnets, and can reach speeds of up to 580 kph (360 mph).

Magnetic Earth

Earth is a giant magnet. It is surrounded by a magnetic field, which is produced by electric currents deep inside the planet's molten metal core. A compass works by sensing Earth's magnetism. It contains a small magnetic needle, and the south pole of the needle points towards Earth's magnetic north pole.

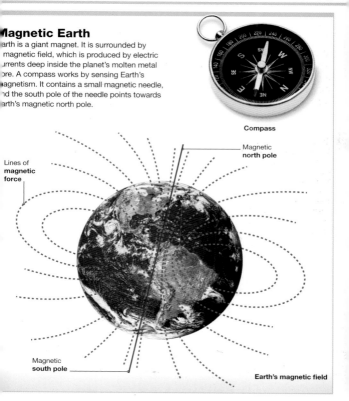

Compass

Magnetic
north pole

Lines of
magnetic
force

Magnetic
south pole

Earth's magnetic field

Electromagnetism

An electrical current always produces a magnetic field around it. Electromagnets are made by passing electricity through a wire that has been wrapped around a piece of iron. Unlike permanent magnets, an electromagnet loses its magnetism as soon as the electrical current is switched off.

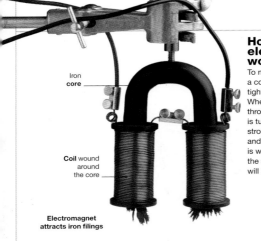

Iron **core**

Coil wound around the core

Electromagnet attracts iron filings

How an electromagnet works

To make an electromagnet, a copper wire is wrapped tightly around an iron core. When electricity passes through the wire, the iron core is turned into a magnet. The stronger the electrical current and the more times the wire is wrapped around the core, the stronger the magnet will be.

Making sounds

Speakers use electromagnets to make sounds. Electricity flows through a small electromagnet inside the speaker. Changes to its magnetic field causes a cone to vibrate. We hear these vibrations as sounds. Varying the strength of the electrical current changes the volume of the sound produced by the speaker.

Magnet produces magnetic field

Wire coil

Cone

Lifting metals

Scrapyards use powerful electromagnets to pick up and move heavy objects. Only magnetic materials such as iron are attracted to the magnet. Electromagnets are also used to separate magnetic metal from non-magnetic materials so that it can be recycled.

Giant **electromagnet** attached to a crane

The EM spectrum

Electromagnetic (EM) radiation is a form of energy that travels in waves at a speed of 300,000 km (186,000 miles) per second, which is the fastest speed in the Universe. Different kinds of radiation make up the EM spectrum. All types of radiation except visible light are invisible.

The spectrum

The EM spectrum is made up of seven major types of radiation, which vary in the length of their waves. The shorter the radiation's wavelength, the higher its energy. The longest waves can be many kilometres long, while the shortest are shorter than a single atom.

Hot objects, including mammals, give off invisible rays of heat called **infrared (IR) waves**.

Low-energy waves

Radio waves have the longest wavelength. Radio and TV broadcasts and Wi-Fi use radio waves.

Microwaves are used to heat food. They are also used by mobile phones.

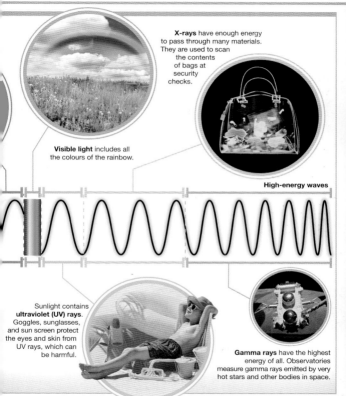

X-rays have enough energy to pass through many materials. They are used to scan the contents of bags at security checks.

Visible light includes all the colours of the rainbow.

High-energy waves

Sunlight contains **ultraviolet (UV) rays**. Goggles, sunglasses, and sun screen protect the eyes and skin from UV rays, which can be harmful.

Gamma rays have the highest energy of all. Observatories measure gamma rays emitted by very hot stars and other bodies in space.

The explosion of the star that formed
the Crab Nebula in 1054 CE was

so bright

that it was visible from
Earth, 62,000 trillion km
(39,000 trillion miles) away

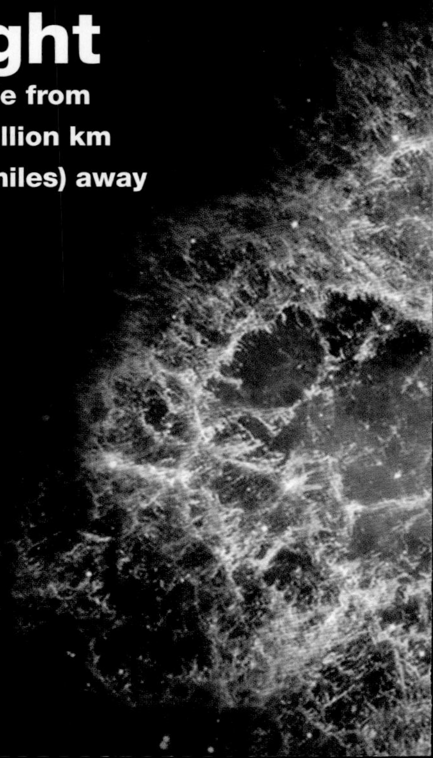

GAMMA RADIATION
The remains of dying stars, such as the Crab Nebula, give out large quantities of radiation, including powerful bursts of gamma rays. Although this nebula is 50 million km (30 million miles) wide, it can now only be seen through a telescope. When it first formed, it could be seen with the naked eye.

Light

Light is the only form of electromagnetic radiation we can see. Most things absorb and reflect light, but few objects give out light. The Sun is the main source of light in the day, while electric lights provide illumination at night.

Making shadows

Some materials, such as glass, allow light to pass through them. They are known as transparent. Other materials, such as wood or metals, do not let light pass through. They are known as opaque. If something blocks the path of light, it creates a dark area behind called a shadow.

A snowboarder blocks the straight path of light creating a shadow

Speed of light

In a vacuum (a space that is empty of all matter), light travels at 300,000 km (186,000 miles) per second. Nothing in the Universe can travel faster. The distances of very far-off objects, such as stars and galaxies, are calculated using the distance light can travel in a year. This distance is known as a light year. One light year equals about 10 trillion km (6 trillion miles).

The Andromeda Galaxy is 2.5 million light years away

Bending and reflecting

Light normally travels in straight lines. When light travels from one material to another, such as when it passes from air to water, its path is bent, or refracted. This can create a distorted image. Light is also bounced, or reflected, by a shiny surface, which sends light back at the same angle at which it hits the surface.

Refraction makes the straw appear bent where it meets the water

Reflection in a mirror

Using light

We need light to see the world and to find our way around it. In the earliest days of humanity, we just used the natural light produced by the Sun and went to bed when it got dark. Today, we can also use artificial lights to illuminate the world.

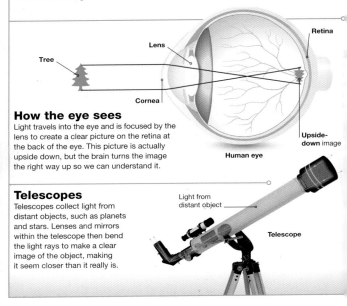

Retina

Lens

Tree

Cornea

Upside-down image

Human eye

How the eye sees

Light travels into the eye and is focused by the lens to create a clear picture on the retina at the back of the eye. This picture is actually upside down, but the brain turns the image the right way up so we can understand it.

Telescopes

Telescopes collect light from distant objects, such as planets and stars. Lenses and mirrors within the telescope then bend the light rays to make a clear image of the object, making it seem closer than it really is.

Light from distant object

Telescope

Camera

Like our eyes, cameras collect and bend light to produce a clear picture. The camera lens focuses light into an image, which is recorded on light-sensitive film or a light-sensitive microchip.

Light is focused by a number of glass lenses to form a sharp image

Lighting the dark

Electric lights convert electrical energy into light. In an incandescent light bulb, this is done by heating a thin piece of metal until it glows. In compact fluorescent lights, electricity is passed through a gas, causing the lamp's phosphor coating to glow and create light.

Electric lights illuminate the city of Penang, Malaysia, at night

Radioactivity

In some atoms, the nucleus changes over time, releasing particles and energy, known as radiation. This process is called radioactive decay. We encounter low-level radiation all the time – in the soil, in the air, and in the food we eat.

Types of radioactivity

There are three types of radioactivity: positively charged alpha particles, which are slow moving and cannot pass through materials easily; negatively charged beta particles, which move much faster; and gamma rays, a form of electromagnetic radiation (see pages 68–69), which carry no charge.

Radioactivity was discovered in 1896 by the French physicist Henri Becquerel when he was investigating X-rays.

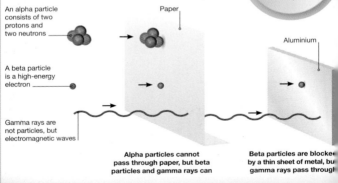

An alpha particle consists of two protons and two neutrons

A beta particle is a high-energy electron

Gamma rays are not particles, but electromagnetic waves

Paper

Aluminium

Alpha particles cannot pass through paper, but beta particles and gamma rays can

Beta particles are blocked by a thin sheet of metal, but gamma rays pass through

Detecting radiation

Radiation is invisible, but it can be detected using a Geiger counter. This simple hand-held device uses a gas-filled tube to measure the presence of alpha particles, beta particles, and gamma rays.

Measuring radiation levels in tomatoes

Using radiation

While high levels of radiation can be harmful, some forms of radioactivity are useful. PET scanners use gamma rays to produce highly detailed images of the inside of the body, which can help doctors to diagnose illnesses.

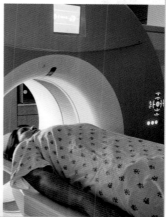

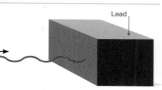

Lead

Gamma rays can be stopped only by a thick layer of dense material, such as lead

Heat

The atoms and molecules that make up matter are always on the move. The more energy they have, the faster they move. We feel this energy as heat. Heat will always move from a warmer area to a colder one until both areas are the same temperature.

Cooling down

The molecules in a hot mug of tea are moving very fast. The tea transfers heat energy to the cooler air. This makes the molecules in the tea slow down, meaning that it gets cooler. After about an hour, the tea and the air will be the same temperature. The colder the air around the mug, the faster the tea will cool down.

This infrared image of a person eating an ice lolly shows the coldest areas in black and warm areas in red and yellow

Detecting heat

Heat energy escapes objects as infrared radiation. Infrared is invisible to our eyes, but special cameras can detect it. Infrared cameras are used by firefighters to see whether there are people trapped in a building, and by the military to see at night.

The balloon is filled with hot, less dense air

Expanding air

When substances heat up, the molecules in them move faster and take up more space. This means that substances expand as they are warmed, and become less dense. To make a hot air balloon float, a burner heats up the air in the balloon. The air inside the balloon is now less dense than the colder air outside it. This causes the balloon to rise.

Measuring temperature

Temperatures are measured using thermometers. Simple thermometers work by measuring the length of a column of liquid. As the temperature increases, the liquid expands and the column becomes longer.

Radiation

Warm objects give off heat in the form of infrared radiation. Earth is warmed by the heat given off by the Sun, which is the hottest object in the Solar System. Infrared lamps can be used to produce heat – the lamp shown here keeps the pigs warm at night.

Convection

Heat can be transferred from one place to another through convection, which is the movement of hot liquid or gas such as air. As air heats up, it becomes less dense and rises. Cooler air sinks and takes its place. This causes convection currents of moving air.

Hang-gliders fly on **convection current** of warm, rising air

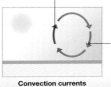

Warm air rises up

Cool air sinks downwards, and is warmed up by heat from the ground

Convection currents

Insulators

Materials that do not allow
heat to pass through them
easily are called insulators.
Plastic, rubber, and wood
are all insulators. Air is also
a good insulator. Fur keeps
animals warm by trapping a layer
of air next to the skin. This stops
heat being removed from the body.

Clothing made from
good insulating material
keeps this climber warm

Conduction

As molecules move, they pass on some of their
heat energy to neighbouring molecules. This
transfer of heat is called conduction. Solids
conduct heat more easily than liquids or gases.
Metals are good conductors and are used to
make saucepans and the base plates of irons.

Sound

Sounds are vibrations that we hear with our ears. The vibrations travel through substances such as air or water in the form of sound waves. When the waves reach our ears, they make our eardrums vibrate. The size and shape of the waves determine the kind of sound we hear.

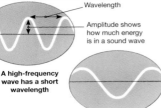

Wavelength

Amplitude shows how much energy is in a sound wave

A high-frequency wave has a short wavelength

A low-frequency wave has a long wavelength

High and low

The number of vibrations a sound wave makes every second is called its frequency. The higher a sound's frequency, the higher its pitch, or note. Some animals, such as dogs, can hear sounds with a very high pitch that humans cannot hear. Elephants can hear very low-pitched sounds.

Using sounds

Sound waves bounce off hard objects. We hear sound bouncing back at us as an echo. Some animals, such as dolphins and bats, use echoes to detect prey. They emit high-pitched sounds and listen out for any echo bouncing back off objects around them.

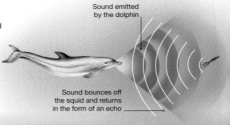

Sound emitted by the dolphin

Sound bounces off the squid and returns in the form of an echo

Sound quality

The quality, or timbre, of a sound is determined by the shape of its wave. Each instrument in an orchestra has a different timbre. Some, such as a flute, produce sound waves with a regular shape, which we hear as a pure note. Others, such as drums, make rougher sounds with irregular waves.

Loud and soft

The more energy a sound wave contains, the larger its amplitude. We hear sounds with lots of energy as loud sounds. A sound's loudness is measured in decibels. Decibels are measured on a special scale called a logarithmic scale. A sound measured at 20 dB is ten times louder than one measured at 10 dB.

The sound of a bomb explosion may hit 200 dB, which is loud enough to damage our ears

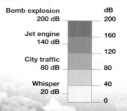

	dB
Bomb explosion 200 dB	200
Jet engine 140 dB	160
	120
City traffic 80 dB	80
	40
Whisper 20 dB	0

Decibel (dB) scale

Forces

Forces are pushes and pulls that change an object's shape or movement. Every time an object speeds up, slows down, or changes direction, this happens because a force is acting on it. Forces such as gravity can act over huge distances, keeping the planets in orbit around the Sun.

Gravity

The force of gravity pulls all objects towards each other. Objects with just a small mass only pull very weakly, but the gravity of our planet Earth is strong enough to hold us to the ground. Space rockets use powerful engines to push them away from the ground and break free from Earth's gravity.

Hot gases are pushed downwards

An equal and opposite force pushes the rocket upwards

A black hole is a very dense object in space. It has such strong gravity, it pulls everything around it, even light from stars.

Atlas V rocket launching into space

Wide tracks spread the weight of the tank over a large area, stopping it from sinking in the sand

Under pressure

A force acting on a particular area causes pressure. A force applied over a small area produces more pressure than the same force applied over a larger area. The tracks on a tank's wheels spread its weight over a large area. This reduces the pressure and stops it from sinking in soft ground.

The force of the person swinging the pickaxe is concentrated on the axe's sharp point, producing enough pressure to split the rock

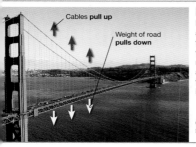

Cables **pull up**

Weight of road **pulls down**

Golden Gate Bridge, San Francisco, USA

Balanced forces

More than one force can act on an object at the same time. Two forces pulling in opposite directions will stretch an object, but will not move it. The cables holding up a suspension bridge pull against the weight of the bridge to stop it from collapsing.

Air resistance

Also called drag, air resistance is a force that pushes against an object as it moves through the air. The faster the object moves, the greater the air resistance, which tries to slow the object down. Jet fighters have a smooth, streamlined shape to reduce air resistance.

Jet fighter in flight

Friction

When two objects rub against each other, the action produces a force called friction. Friction slows down movement and generates heat. The brakes in cars use friction to slow their wheels down by pressing a disc against them.

Brake disc glows because of heat caused by friction

Streamlined shape reduces air resistance

Thin wings are designed to let air flow smoothly around them without producing too much air resistance

Reducing friction

Friction is caused when the rough surfaces of objects catch one another as the objects rub against each other. Rolling movement reduces friction because a rolling object rubs much less against the flat surface it is rolling on.

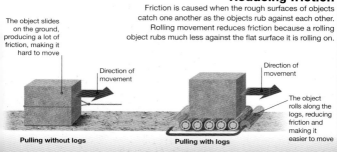

The object slides on the ground, producing a lot of friction, making it hard to move

Direction of movement

Direction of movement

The object rolls along the logs, reducing friction and making it easier to move

Pulling without logs

Pulling with logs

Forces and movement

Whenever an object changes speed or direction, this happens because a force is acting on it. More than 300 years ago, the English scientist Isaac Newton worked out three laws of motion that explain how forces affect movement.

First law of motion

The first law states that an object will continue at the same velocity in a straight line if no force is acting on it. If the object is not moving, it will remain at rest until a force acts on it. The space probe *Voyager 2* is flying through space with almost no forces acting on it to slow it down, so it will carry on moving at the same velocity.

Second law of motion

According to Newton's second law, the greater the force applied, the greater the acceleration. Acceleration also depends on the mass of the object – the more mass it has, the more force is needed to accelerate it. Motorcycles have much smaller mass than cars, and can accelerate very quickly.

VELOCITY AND ACCELERATION

An object's velocity is the speed at which it is travelling in a particular direction. An increase in velocity is called acceleration, while a decrease is called deceleration. Racing cars have powerful engines and can accelerate to high speeds incredibly quickly – from 0 to 160 kph (100 mph) in under 5 seconds.

Third law of motion

Newton's third law of motion states that every action has an equal and opposite reaction. A jet engine attached to an aircraft burns fuel to send out a powerful stream of hot gases behind it. As this jet of gases shoots backwards, it pushes the engine forwards, and the aircraft with it.

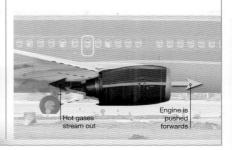

Hot gases stream out

Engine is pushed forwards

Wind speeds in a tornado can reach more than

480 kph

(300 mph), strong enough to tear down trees and send cars flying through the air

THE FORCES OF WIND
Tornadoes are violently destructive storms that form from rotating blocks of air in thunderclouds. As the hot air rises and the cold air sinks, the two blocks begin to spin, forming a rotating column of super-fast winds.

Simple machines

We use simple machines to help us do our work more easily.
There are six kinds of simple machine. They change the
direction or size of a force, allowing us to use less effort
when moving, separating, or keeping heavy objects in place.

Inclined planes

An inclined plane, or ramp, is a sloping
surface. It reduces the force needed to lift
an object by increasing the distance it has
to travel. A screw is an inclined plane
wrapped around a cylinder, which
moves in a circle.

Inclined plane

Screw

Distance travelled

Height raised

Wedges

A wedge is a triangular-shaped
machine. It changes a force applied
to its blunt end into a force that
pushes outwards. Wedges can
be used to cut through objects –
as with an axe cutting through
wood – or to hold objects in place,
like a wedge holding open a door.

Blunt end

Wheels

A wheel is a machine attached to a central shaft, or axle. The axle and wheel turn together. Monster trucks have huge wheels, which allow them to ride over large obstacles, including cars. Each turn of the wheels moves the truck a long distance.

Gears

Gears are wheels with teeth. Connected together, gears transfer a force from one place to another and can change the size of the force. Here, the larger yellow gear is twice the size of the smaller blue one. So, for every complete turn of the yellow gear, the blue gear turns twice.

Levers

Simple machines called levers make it easier to lift heavy loads. A lever is fixed at one point, called the fulcrum, and rotates around that point. There are three different classes of lever, depending on the position of the fulcrum, the load, and the effort needed to lift the load.

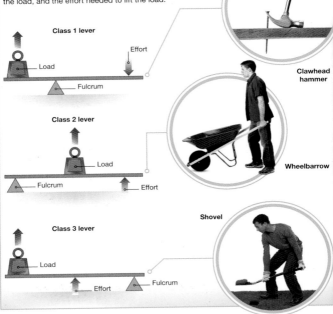

Class 1 lever

Effort

Load

Fulcrum

Clawhead hammer

Class 2 lever

Load

Fulcrum

Effort

Wheelbarrow

Shovel

Class 3 lever

Load

Effort

Fulcrum

Wheel · Axle

Load moves up

Effort pulls down

Load

Load

Working of a pulley system

Pulleys

A pulley is a wheel on an axle with a rope running around it. A single pulley on its own can change the direction of a force. Two or more pulleys working together reduce the amount of force needed to lift a load by increasing the distance the rope has to travel.

Pulley system being used in a weight-training exercise

Complex machines

Simple machines can be combined to make complex machines. A pair of scissors is a complex machine that combines two types of simple machine – the blades as wedges and the handles as levers. The Space Shuttle was probably the most complex machine ever built, with more than 2.5 million separate parts.

Jib

Pulley

Crane

A mobile crane combines three simple machines to pick up loads and move them. The load is lifted vertically using pulleys, which are attached to a jib. The jib acts as a lever. The crane is mounted on wheels so it can move around.

Engine

**Illustration of
a Formula One car
with driver inside**

20

Axle

Wheel

Brake
disc

Car

A car contains many simple machines.
The wheels are attached to a gearbox, which
allows the car to move at different speeds. The driver
changes gears by pulling on the gearstick, which is
a lever. The engine changes the energy from burning
fuel into movements that turn the wheels.

Boring drill

A boring drill is a machine used to
make deep holes in the ground. The drill
bit is a screw with a sharp wedge on
one end. A powerful engine turns the
drill bit using a large force so that it can
cut through hard ground and rock.

Drill bit

Computers

A computer is a machine that can be programmed to perform a huge range of tasks. Computers work using simple electronic circuits, called transistors, which can only be turned on or off. Millions of transistors can be combined to form microprocessors, which process instructions and tell the computer what to do.

Early computers

Scientists in the UK and the USA developed the first programmable electronic computers during World War II. With circuits made up of bulky wire and valves, these early computers were huge, often filling entire rooms.

ENIAC, an early computer

Microchip

Computers began to get smaller and faster following the invention of the microchip in the late 1950s. A microchip is a small piece of semiconducting material, such as silicon (see page 35), on to which millions of tiny circuits have been traced.

Computer chip

Modern computers

Modern computers are much smaller and millions of times more powerful than the earliest computers. Packed with microchips, they can process millions of instructions in the blink of an eye, allowing them to run applications, take pictures, operate phones, surf the Web, and play games all at the same time.

A tablet computer is operated by touching the screen

Artificial intelligence

Even the most powerful computers have to be programmed – they can do only what people tell them to do. But some experts believe that computers will one day become so advanced that computers and robots will have artificial intelligence – they will be able to think for themselves and learn from their mistakes.

Humanoid (humanlike) robot Rollin' Justin preparing tea

The living world

Earth is the only place in the Universe where life is known to exist. Millions of different kinds of life form are found all over the planet. Some, such as bacteria, are too small to see with the naked eye, while others, such as trees, may be more than 100 m (330 ft) tall. Many habitats are incredibly rich in life – from lush tropical forests teeming with insects, mammals, and frogs to coral reefs on the sea floor, which are packed with brightly coloured fish, crustaceans, and tiny plankton.

WHAT IS LIFE?
Living things are organized structures that reproduce themselves. Viruses can only reproduce inside other living things, so they are not usually thought of as alive.

Types of living thing

Scientists divide the wide variety of life on Earth into different groups. The smallest group is the "species", which are life forms that are very similar, and are able to breed with each other. The largest group is the "kingdom". There are five kingdoms – fungi, bacteria, protists, plants, and animals.

Fungi

A group of living things called fungi feeds on dead or rotting animals and plants. This kingdom includes mushrooms, moulds, and yeast.

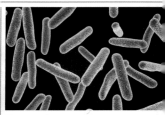

Bacteria

All living things are made up of microscopic units called cells. Tiny single-celled bacteria are the simplest form of life, and the most common. They are found all over the planet.

Plants

Members of the plant kingdom produce oxygen and are crucial to life on Earth. They make their own food using the energy of the Sun, and also provide food for both animals and fungi.

Protists

The protists are also single-celled life forms. Their cells are more complex than bacteria, and contain a nucleus as a control centre. Many protists, such as algae, live together in large groups.

Zebras and wildebeest are mammals, a kind of vertebrate

Animals

The animal kingdom is divided into two groups: vertebrates, which have a backbone and include mammals, reptiles, and fish; and invertebrates, which lack a backbone and include insects, spiders, and crustaceans.

Classifying life

In order to study the wide range of life on Earth, scientists group together living things that have similar characteristics. There are different levels of groups depending on how similar the life forms are. The broadest level is a kingdom, such as animals. All animals are then divided into smaller and smaller groups until a single species is identified.

What is a species?

A species is a group of very similar living things that usually breed with one other. Each species is identified by a scientific name. The European larch tree has the scientific name *Larix decidua*. It belongs to a family of trees called Pinaceae, which all produce cones.

Class: Mammals
A class is a large group within a phylum. Mammals are warm-blooded vertebrates that feed their young on milk.

Phylum: Chordates
Within the animal kingdom are 35 phyla (plural of phylum). The phylum Chordates contains vertebrates, animals with a backbone.

Kingdom: Animals
The largest group is a kingdom. The animal kingdom contains all the animals in the world.

Start here

Species: *Canis lupis*
The grey wolf is the largest species in the family Canidae. Its scientific name is *Canis lupis*.

Genus: *Canis*
Families contain different genera (plural of genus). The genus *Canis* contains 10 species, including wolves and domestic dogs.

Family: Canidae
Within the order of carnivores, the family Canidae contains all doglike mammals.

Order: Carnivores
A class is divided into orders. The order of carnivores contains mammals that eat meat.

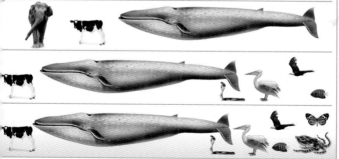

Microlife

Bacteria and protists are single-celled organisms that can only be seen using a microscope. Bacteria are so small that 10,000 could fit on the head of a pin. Microlife is found all around us, and even inside us – there are ten times as many bacteria in our bodies as there are cells!

Colony of *Noctiluca scintillans*, a sea-living protist

Protists

These single-celled organisms are found anywhere there is water. Some, such as protozoa, move around and feed on other protists or on bacteria. Others, such as algae, make their own food using the energy of the Sun, like plants. Sometimes protists come together in huge colonies of billions of individual cells.

Good bacteria

Special bacteria in our stomachs help us to digest food. We can also use bacteria to make our food. The varied flavours of different kinds of cheese are produced with the help of bacteria.

Bad bacteria

Diseases such as cholera and tetanus are caused by harmful bacteria. We protect ourselves from these bacteria with vaccines. A vaccine is a safe dose of a less harmful form of the bacteria that make us ill. This makes our bodies produce antibodies, special proteins that will fight off the harmful forms if they ever appear in the future.

Vaccines are often given as injections

Fungi

Fungi are life forms such as mushrooms, yeasts, and moulds that feed on plants and animals. They break down dead animals and plants, feeding on the nutrients. When the fungi die and are themselves eaten, this recycles the nutrients.

Mushrooms

The familiar mushrooms that grow in fields are just a small part of a fungus that grows underground. The mushrooms are the "fruiting body" of the fungus – they produce and scatter spores, which grow into new fungi. Some mushrooms are edible, but many are poisonous.

After being eaten, mushrooms containing a chemical called psilocybin can cause hallucinations.

Mushrooms release **spores** into the air from their gills

Yeast

Yeast is a tiny single-celled fungus. It feeds on sugars, producing carbon dioxide gas and alcohol. Yeast is used in the making of bread, and the carbon dioxide it produces makes the bread rise. The alcohol evaporates away as the bread is baked.

Yeast mixture

Yeast helps dough to rise

Dough

Moulds

Moulds are microscopic fungi that grow in thin strands called hyphae. They feed on dead plants and animals, making them rot. In medicine, a mould called *Penicillium* produces penicillin (see page 9), a valuable antibiotic for treating infections.

Mould grows on stale food

Plants

Plants range in size from enormous trees to tiny mosses. They make their own food using the energy of the Sun in a process called photosynthesis. Most plants are fixed in one place, with roots that can go deep into the ground. There are many different groups of plant, including ferns, mosses, flowering plants, and conifers.

Flower

Leaf

Stem

Root

Plant parts

Every part of a plant has a job to do. The roots hold the plant in place and also take in water and nutrients from the soil. These are transferred to the rest of the plant through the stem, which also supports the leaves and flowers. Flowers produce pollen, seeds, and fruit, which are used for reproduction.

Ferns

Ferns do not make flowers, but reproduce by releasing spores into the air from the surface of special leaves. Ferns are often found in damp, shady woods, but also grow on rock faces, in wetlands, and even on the sides of trees.

Mosses

Mosses are small plants that are 1–10 cm (0.4–4 in) tall. They grow in clumps in damp, shady areas. Mosses are very simple plants with small leaves attached to wiry stems. They do not have roots or grow flowers.

Flowering plants

The biggest group of plants, flowering plants range from mighty oak trees to the tiny duckweed, just 1 mm (0.005 in) long. They produce flowers, fruit, and seeds. The flowers often have brilliant colours and attract insects and birds, which carry pollen from one plant to another, fertilizing them.

Conifers

Many trees are flowering plants. However, conifers do not produce flowers and grow cones to store their seeds instead. These trees have needle-shaped leaves and mostly grow in huge forests in cold parts of the world.

Redwood trees
can live for more than
3,000 years

GIANT REDWOODS
The largest tree species in the world is the giant redwood, which grows in California, USA. Hyperion, the tallest redwood, stands 115.5 m (379 ft) tall. Chandelier tree is about 20 m (65 ft) shorter, but has a hole in its trunk that is 1.8 m (6 ft) wide – big enough to drive cars through.

How plants work

Unlike animals, plants make their own food. They do this during the daytime, when they use sunlight to provide energy for the food-making process, called photosynthesis. This takes place in the plant's leaves, using a green chemical called chlorophyll.

Surviving winter

In cool parts of the world, plants stop growing in winter. Many trees no longer make their own food and so stop producing chlorophyll. Their leaves turn from green to brown before falling off. This allows them to save energy and stops them from losing water through the leaves.

Dragonfly trapped insid[e] a Venus flytra[p]

Meat-eaters

In places with poor soil, such as bogs, plants can find it hard to get all the nutrients they need. Carnivorous plants have solved this problem by eating meat. The Venus flytrap has specially adapted leaves that tempt insects in, then snap shut as soon as they land, trapping the animals.

The Venus flytrap's leaves snap shut only when living prey lands on them. They will not close if hit by raindrops.

Photosynthesis

Leaves contain a special green chemical called chlorophyll. Chlorophyll is crucial to photosynthesis as it absorbs sunlight and uses the energy to make food from carbon dioxide in the air and water drawn up from the roots. This process produces oxygen, which is released into the air.

Sunlight is absorbed by the plant

Plant gives out oxygen

Plant takes in carbon dioxide

Chloroplasts are tiny structures that contain chlorophyll. They are found inside the cells of leaves.

Chloroplast

Leaf cell

Roots absorb water from the ground

Flowers and seeds

Most plants reproduce using seeds. The seeds are made when the male part (pollen) of one plant combines with the female part (ovum) of another plant. The plant then scatters its seeds to new places, where they take root and grow into new plants.

Mexican hat plant drops buds to reproduce

Reproducing alone

Some plants, such as the Mexican hat plant, can reproduce without making seeds. They reproduce by growing buds that drop to the ground to grow into new plants. The new plants are identical to their parent. This process is called asexual reproduction.

Flowers

Most flowers make both pollen and ova (male and female parts) but cannot fertilize themselves (make their own seeds). Instead, the pollen from one flower is carried to other flowers on the bodies of insects and other animals, or by the wind. The pollen fertilizes the ova, which then develop into seeds.

Pollen gets stuck to a bee's body when it visits a flower to collect nectar

SCATTERING SEEDS

Wind can blow away seeds

Animals eat fruits and disperse seeds

Plants spread their seeds in different ways. The flowers may grow into fruit, which are eaten by animals. The seeds then fall to the ground in the animals' droppings. Some plants make sticky seeds called burrs, which stick to animal fur. Others use the wind, rivers, or oceans to carry their seeds away.

Seeds can be carried away by water

Seeds may stick to fur of animals passing by

Germinating

When a seed lands in the right place and conditions to grow into a new plant, it germinates. A shoot grows out of the seed and develops into a stem that grows upwards and a root that grows downwards. Food inside the seed gives it the energy to begin germinating, but it soon starts to make its own food in its leaves by photosynthesis.

Germination of a bean seed

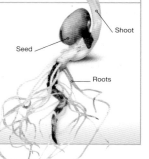

Shoot

Seed

Roots

What is an animal?

Animals are living things that get their energy by feeding on other living things, including plants and other animals. Like plants, animals can respond and react to the world around them and communicate with each other. Most animals can also move around. Animals range from simple, tubelike sponges to complex human beings.

On the move

A few animals, such as sponges and clams, fix themselves in one place, but most need to move to find food or shelter. Sharks have powerful muscles and a sleek body shape, which allows them to swim through the water quickly in search of prey.

A shark looking for food

Feeding

All animals obtain energy by eating other living things. Herbivores eat plants, while carnivores eat other animals. Humans are omnivores, which are animals that eat both plants and other animals.

A cow is a herbivore

A crocodile is a carnivore

A bear is an omnivore

Responding and reacting

Animals have sense organs that tell them what is going on outside their bodies. For example, hairs on a spider's feet sense vibrations when prey gets trapped in its web. The spider then runs over and wraps its prey in silk.

Communication

Animals communicate with each other in different ways: using sounds, chemicals, colours, or movements. Bees tell others in their hive where to find food using a special dance, which shows which way to fly and how long it will take to get there.

Octopuses have

three hearts –

two to pump blood to their
gills and one to pump blood
around the body

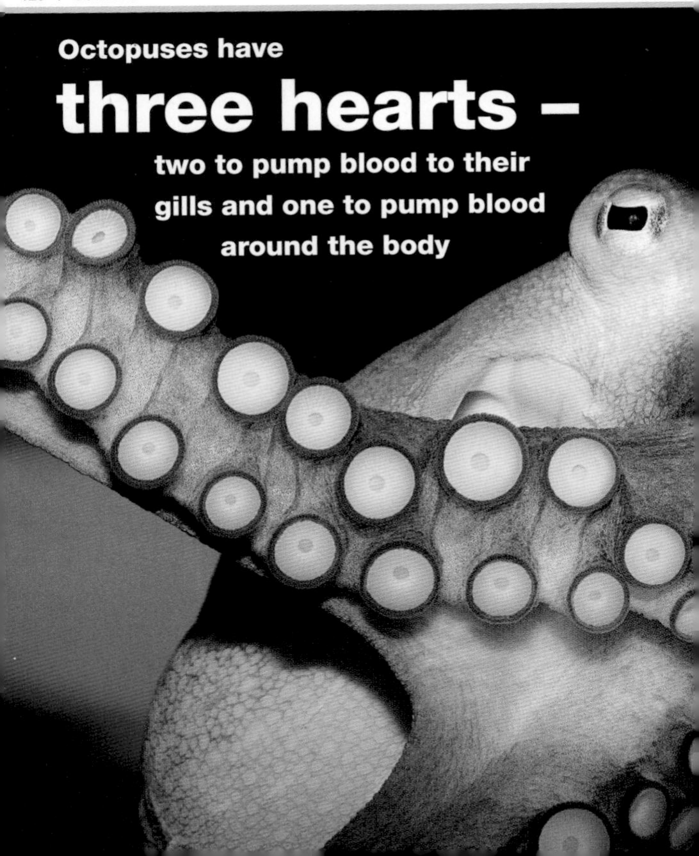

ARMED AND DANGEROUS
The octopus lives in holes and crevices on the ocean floor. It has eight arms, lined with suction cups for grabbing hold of its prey, which it then kills with poison from its beak. If it loses an arm, it can grow another one.

Types of animal

There are millions of animal species living on Earth. They are divided into two main groups: vertebrates, such as mammals and fish, which have a backbone; and invertebrates, such as insects and molluscs, which do not have a backbone.

VERTEBRATES

There are five main groups of vertebrates – amphibians, reptiles, fish, birds, and mammals. They all have internal skeletons but come in all shapes and sizes and live in very varied places.

Amphibians, such as frogs, lay their eggs in water and live both in the water and on land.

Reptiles, including alligators, have scaly skin and lay their eggs on land.

Fish, such as goldfish, spend all their lives in water, where they can breathe using gills.

Birds, including eagles, have feathers and many of them can fly.

Mammals are warm blooded, have hairy skin, and feed their young on milk. They include tigers and humans.

INVERTEBRATES

About 97 per cent of all known animal species are invertebrates. Insects and crustaceans have hard external skeletons and bodies made from segments. Starfish have simple bodies with bony plates just under the skin, while soft-bodied worms and squid do not have a skeleton at all.

Anthozoa, such as coral, fix themselves in one place and feed on algae or plankton.

Asterozoa, including starfish, are star-shaped, with arms growing out of a central disc.

Arachnids have eight legs, which have joints. They include spiders and scorpions.

Gastropods include snails and slugs. They move around using one muscular foot.

Insects have six legs, and many have two pairs of wings. They include butterflies and ants.

Malacostraca, such as crabs, have shells and heads made of five segments.

Animal reproduction

Animals use different methods to reproduce (have babies). The young of some species develop inside eggs laid by the mother, while other species give birth. Some have many young, most of which will be eaten by predators, while others produce few offspring, which they look after carefully.

Laying eggs

Chick hatching

Many animals lay eggs. Fish and amphibians lay their eggs in water. Their eggs do not have shells and are soft. Reptiles' eggs have leathery shells, while birds' eggs have hard shells. The shells protect the eggs and stop them from drying out. The baby reptiles or birds must break through the shell when they hatch.

Eggs galore

Some animals, including many amphibians and fish, lay thousands of eggs. They leave the eggs, so the young have to fend for themselves as soon as they hatch. Most of the eggs and young will be eaten before they grow up, but a few of them survive to adulthood.

Mass of frogspawn (frog's eggs)

Live young

Most mammals give birth to live young. The babies develop inside their mothers and receive all the nutrients they need to grow from their mother's blood. After they are born, the young feed on their mother's milk as they continue to grow.

Looking after babies

Some parents look after their young for months or even years after they are born. The parents bring food for the young and teach them the skills they will need to survive. Lions live in groups and help each other care for the young.

Lioness tends to her cubs

Food webs

Energy passes from one living thing to another in the form of food. Food webs show how living things feed on one another. At the bottom of a food web are plants, which make their own food using energy from the Sun. At the top are predators, which feed on other animals.

Deer are **primary consumers**, which feed on grass

Lions are **secondary consumers**, which feed on deer

Decomposers, such as dung beetles, feed on droppings and the bodies of dead animals

Grasses are **producers**, which make their own food by photosynthesis

Food chain

Food webs are made up of many different food chains, which have different levels. In a food chain, plants are called producers because they make their own food. Animals that eat plants are called primary consumers. Primary consumers are eaten by other animals called secondary consumers, or predators. When all living things die, they become the food of organisms called decomposers.

Food pyramid

As we go up a food chain, the amount of food available decreases. This is because living things use most of the energy in the food they eat in respiration (see page 128). A food pyramid shows how energy is lost at each level. Near the top, there are just a few predators, while at the bottom there are many more producers.

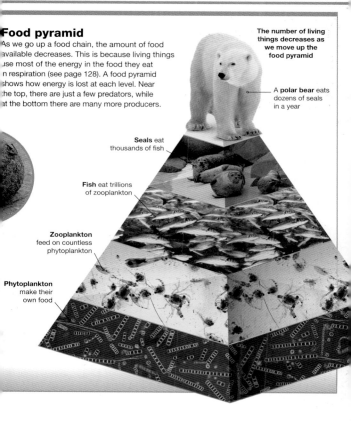

The number of living things decreases as we move up the food pyramid

A **polar bear** eats dozens of seals in a year

Seals eat thousands of fish

Fish eat trillions of zooplankton

Zooplankton feed on countless phytoplankton

Phytoplankton make their own food

Cycles

Every living thing needs the elements oxygen and carbon to grow and make energy. These elements are constantly passing from the air into living things and back into the air again in cycles that are essential to life.

The oxygen cycle

Plants release oxygen into the air and absorb carbon dioxide from the air during photosynthesis (see page 115), which occurs only during the day. Both animals and plants use the oxygen in air to release energy in their bodies during a process called respiration. Respiration takes place all the time and produces carbon dioxide, which is released into the air to be absorbed by plants during photosynthesis as the cycle is repeated.

➡ Oxygen

➡ Carbon dioxide

Plants take in carbon dioxide and give out oxygen during **photosynthesis**

Plants take in oxygen and give out carbon dioxide all the time as they **respire**

Animals breathe in oxygen and breathe out carbon dioxide all the time as they **respire**

The carbon cycle

Carbon is taken in by living things in their food. It is released into the atmosphere during respiration and also when plants and animals die and decay. During photosynthesis, plants absorb carbon dioxide from the atmosphere so they can grow, which will provide new food for other living things.

Plants **give out carbon dioxide** during respiration

Carbon dioxide in the atmosphere

Animals **breathe out carbon dioxide** and their **dung** also contains carbon

Plants **take in carbon dioxide** during photosynthesis

Animals **eat plants** and take in some carbon

Decomposers, such as worms, bacteria, and fungi, **give out carbon dioxide** as they feed and respire

Plants and animals die and their bodies **decay**

Ecosystems

A community of organisms that lives in a particular environment is called an ecosystem. A single ecosystem might be as small as a pond or as large as a desert. Ecosystems vary hugely across the world depending on conditions such as climate, the soil type, or whether there is salt or fresh water.

Tundra is found near polar regions and high up on mountains, where it is too cold for trees and so only small flowers and grasses grow. It covers one-fifth of Earth's land.

NORTH AMERICA

Grasslands are wide areas that are baked brown by the Sun in summer and may freeze over in winter. They are covered with grasses and have few trees.

SOUTH AMERICA

Rainforests have a thick covering of trees and a rich variety of animal life.

Mountains are high places with a cold, windy climate. Very different groups of plants and animals are found at different heights, as the climate changes rapidly between the peaks and the valleys.

KEY

- Polar regions
- Mountains
- Rainforests
- Coniferous forests
- Temperate forests
- Wetlands
- Grasslands
- Tundra
- Deserts
- Oceans

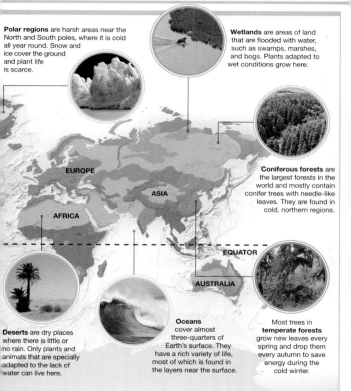

Polar regions are harsh areas near the North and South poles, where it is cold all year round. Snow and ice cover the ground and plant life is scarce.

Wetlands are areas of land that are flooded with water, such as swamps, marshes, and bogs. Plants adapted to wet conditions grow here.

Coniferous forests are the largest forests in the world and mostly contain conifer trees with needle-like leaves. They are found in cold, northern regions.

EUROPE

ASIA

AFRICA

EQUATOR

AUSTRALIA

Deserts are dry places where there is little or no rain. Only plants and animals that are specially adapted to the lack of water can live here.

Oceans cover almost three-quarters of Earth's surface. They have a rich variety of life, most of which is found in the layers near the surface.

Most trees in **temperate forests** grow new leaves every spring and drop them every autumn to save energy during the cold winter.

The Great Barrier Reef is 2,600 km (1,600 miles) long, and is so large that it can be

seen from space

TEEMING WITH LIFE
Coral reefs found in shallow, tropical waters are some of the most diverse habitats on Earth. Although they cover just 0.1 per cent of the oceans, they are home to 25 per cent of ocean species, including molluscs, sea snakes, crustaceans, and many kinds of colourful fish.

Survival

Living things have a wide range of methods to find food, keep themselves safe from predators, and survive changing conditions. These include living in large groups, moving from place to place, and even feeding off other animals.

Symbiosis

Sometimes two different species of plant or animal live with each other in a way that helps both of them. This is called symbiosis. Clownfish have a symbiotic partnership with anemones. The anemones provide the fish with protection and food. In return, the fish defend the anemones from predators and keep them clean.

Clownfish

Anemone

Head louse as seen under a scanning electron microscope (SEM)

Parasites

Some living things, called parasites, live off others in a way that harms or even kills them. Head lice live in human hair, and feed on our blood. They do not kill us, but they make our scalps very itchy.

Safety in numbers

Some animals travel together in large groups. This makes it harder for predators to catch them, and may also help them catch their own food. Fish such as herring form huge groups, called shoals, that may number hundreds of millions of individuals.

Migration

Animals may move from one region to another to find food or places to reproduce. This is called migration. Monarch butterflies migrate from Canada to Mexico every autumn, and back again every spring. Each migration takes three or four generations, so no individual insect survives the whole trip.

Living in water

Creatures that live in oceans or rivers are specially adapted to move, breathe, and feed in water. The oceans contain a wide variety of animal life, from tiny plankton to the gigantic blue whale.

Breathing under water

Fish, such as this stingray, and many other sea creatures breathe the oxygen dissolved in water using organs called gills. Some small creatures absorb oxygen through their skin without using gills.

Gill flap

Water flows in through the fish's mouth and over the **gills**, which absorb oxygen from the water

Hold your breath

Sea-dwelling reptiles, such as turtles, and mammals, such as whales, do not have gills. They have to come to the surface to breathe. Killer whales breathe through blowholes at the top of their heads. They can dive and hold their breath for up to 20 minutes.

Jet-propelled

Some invertebrates, such as an octopus, move through the water using jet propulsion. They suck water into their bodies and force it out behind them in a strong jet that pushes them forwards.

Big creatures

As the weight of their bodies is supported by the water, animals in the oceans can grow to enormous sizes. The biggest of them all, the blue whale, can grow to some 30 m (100 ft) long and weigh more than 180 tonnes.

Flying

Animals that spend much of their time in the air fly using wings. Most flying insects have two pairs of wings attached to their bodies, while birds and bats fly using wings that are specially adapted arms.

Bats' wings are made of skin

Bats flying out of a cave

Insect wings are made of a substance called chitin

Beetle in flight

Geese in flight

Wings

For animals to fly, they need to produce an upwards force called lift. They do this using their wings, which are a special shape called an aerofoil. They flap their wings to give them more lift, but once in the air, many birds can also fly without flapping.

Hollow bones

Flying uses a lot of energy, so it is important for flying animals to be as light as possible. Birds' bones are hollow, which makes their skeletons very light.

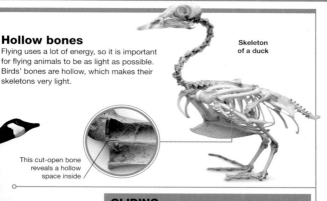

Skeleton of a duck

This cut-open bone reveals a hollow space inside

Birds' wings are made of feathers

GLIDING

Some animals do not truly fly, but can glide long distances through the air. They use flat parts of their bodies like a parachute to slow their fall. Flying squirrels stretch out flaps of skin attached to their front and back legs to glide from one tree to another.

Evolution

Over millions of years, living things change in response to changes in their environment. This is called evolution and it happens through a process called natural selection. Changes that are more likely to help a plant or animal survive are passed to future generations, but living things with changes that are not suited to survival die out.

Adaptation

Natural selection has produced living things that are superbly adapted to life in the places they live in. Species that have adaptations better suited to an environment are more likely to survive than those that do not. Plants in deserts need to be able to save water, while animals in the Arctic need to survive the cold.

Cactus stores water to survive in dry conditions

Polar bear has thick fur that helps in surviving the cold temperatures

Human evolution

Humans evolved from apelike ancestors over millions of years. In that time, different species evolved and were replaced until modern humans first appeared about 200,000 years ago.

Homo heidelbergensis
(500,000 years ago)

Australopithecus afarensis
(3 million years ago)

Ardipithecus ramidus
(4.5 million years ago)

Homo habilis
(2 million years ago)

Homo erectus
(1.5 million years ago)

Homo sapiens
(200,000 years ago)

Extinction

Changes to the environment, such as climate change, can lead to the disappearance of a whole species, a process called extinction. Extinction is an important part of the evolution process because it gives other species the chance to replace extinct ones.

The dinosaur *Corythosaurus* became extinct about 75 million years ago

Human influence

Human activity is changing environments across the world. We are damaging many natural habitats to meet our growing demands for food, energy, land, and other resources. We are also adding carbon dioxide to the atmosphere by burning fossil fuels such as oil, and this is changing our atmosphere and may be causing global warming.

Habitat destruction

Many forests have been cut down to make use of the wood and to clear land for agriculture. This destroys the forest habitats and also reduces the number of trees in the world. Trees take carbon dioxide from the air, so cutting them down increases the level of this gas in the atmosphere, contributing to dangerous climate change.

Deforestation in Peru

Reducing the impact

There are many ways in which we can reduce the impact of human activity. By planting trees, we replace the ones that have been cut down. We can also reduce our impact by recycling (using again) anything we might normally throw away.

Conservation

The destruction of habitats has left many species of plant and animal endangered. This means that they are close to becoming extinct. Scientists and conservationists study how these species live and grow to see how they can be saved from extinction.

Scientists check on the health of a loggerhead turtle, an endangered species

The periodic table

Elements are pure chemicals that cannot be broken down further (see page 32). The atoms in different elements contain different amounts of protons, neutrons, and electrons, which affects their chemistry. Elements are arranged in a system called the periodic table according to their chemical and physical properties.

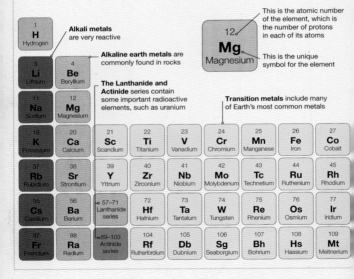

Alkali metals are very reactive

Alkaline earth metals are commonly found in rocks

The **Lanthanide** and **Actinide** series contain some important radioactive elements, such as uranium

This is the atomic number of the element, which is the number of protons in each of its atoms

This is the unique symbol for the element

Transition metals include many of Earth's most common metals

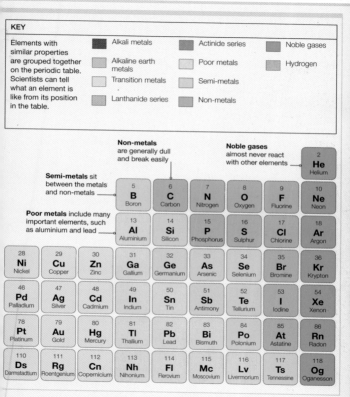

KEY

Elements with similar properties are grouped together on the periodic table. Scientists can tell what an element is like from its position in the table.

- Alkali metals
- Alkaline earth metals
- Transition metals
- Lanthanide series
- Actinide series
- Poor metals
- Semi-metals
- Non-metals
- Noble gases
- Hydrogen

Non-metals are generally dull and break easily

Noble gases almost never react with other elements

Semi-metals sit between the metals and non-metals

Poor metals include many important elements, such as aluminium and lead

| 2 **He** Helium |

| 5 **B** Boron | 6 **C** Carbon | 7 **N** Nitrogen | 8 **O** Oxygen | 9 **F** Fluorine | 10 **Ne** Neon |

| 13 **Al** Aluminium | 14 **Si** Silicon | 15 **P** Phosphorus | 16 **S** Sulphur | 17 **Cl** Chlorine | 18 **Ar** Argon |

| 28 **Ni** Nickel | 29 **Cu** Copper | 30 **Zn** Zinc | 31 **Ga** Gallium | 32 **Ge** Germanium | 33 **As** Arsenic | 34 **Se** Selenium | 35 **Br** Bromine | 36 **Kr** Krypton |

| 46 **Pd** Palladium | 47 **Ag** Silver | 48 **Cd** Cadmium | 49 **In** Indium | 50 **Sn** Tin | 51 **Sb** Antimony | 52 **Te** Tellurium | 53 **I** Iodine | 54 **Xe** Xenon |

| 78 **Pt** Platinum | 79 **Au** Gold | 80 **Hg** Mercury | 81 **Tl** Thallium | 82 **Pb** Lead | 83 **Bi** Bismuth | 84 **Po** Polonium | 85 **At** Astatine | 86 **Rn** Radon |

| 110 **Ds** Darmstadtium | 111 **Rg** Roentgenium | 112 **Cn** Copernicium | 113 **Nh** Nihonium | 114 **Fl** Flerovium | 115 **Mc** Moscovium | 116 **Lv** Livermorium | 117 **Ts** Tennessine | 118 **Og** Oganesson |

Amazing science facts

MOST COMMON ELEMENTS

- **In the Universe:**
Hydrogen – 75%
Helium – 23%
Other elements – 2%

- **In Earth's crust:**
Oxygen – 47%
Silicon – 28%
Aluminium – 8%
Iron – 5%
Calcium – 4%
Sodium – 3%
Potassium – 3%
Magnesium – 2%

- **In the human body:**
Oxygen – 61%
Carbon – 23%
Hydrogen – 10%
Other elements – 6%

RAREST ELEMENT

- **The rarest element** naturally occurring on Earth is francium. Only about 25 g (1 oz) of francium exists on Earth at any one time. It is highly radioactive, and turns into other elements just minutes after it has formed.

MASSIVE MOLECULES

- **The largest man-made molecule**, PG5, is made up of thousands of carbon, hydrogen, and oxygen atoms bonded together. One molecule of PG5 has the same mass as 200 million hydrogen atoms.

- **The largest molecules found in space** are made of 60 carbon atoms joined together in patterns of hexagons and pentagons, like a football.

- **One strand of DNA**, the molecule that contains the code for life, can contain as many as 220 million pairs of instructions.

Of the 118 elements known to scientists, only 94 elements are found naturally on Earth.

SPEED RECORDS

- **The fastest-moving stuff** in the Universe is light. A particle of light, called a photon, travels 299,792,458 m (983,571,056 ft) every second.

- **The fastest animal** is the peregrine falcon, which reaches speeds of 325 kph (200 mph) when it dives on its prey.

• **The fastest land animal** is the cheetah, which can run at 114 kph (71 mph).

• **The fastest fish** is the sailfish, which can swim at 110 kph (68 mph).

• **The fastest unpowered human** was skydiver Felix Baumgartner who, on 14 October 2012, reached a top speed of 1,342 kph (834 mph) when he jumped from a high-altitude balloon. He was the first human to travel faster than the speed of sound without a powered vehicle.

• **The fastest manned aircraft** was the Lockheed SR-71 Blackbird, which was clocked at 3,530 kph (2,193 mph). Spacecraft are even faster – the Space Shuttles have travelled at 28,000 kph (17,400 mph) when orbiting Earth.

• **The fastest passenger train** is the JR-Maglev, an experimental Japanese train that has reached a top speed of 581 kph (361 mph) in test runs.

• **The fastest unmanned train** is a rocket sled. Powered by rockets, these can slide along rails at more than 10,000 kph (6,200 mph).

• **The water speed record** is 511 kph (317 mph). The record was set in 1978 by Ken Warby in a specially designed boat called *Spirit of Australia*.

ENERGY MATTERS

• **The largest power station** in the world is the hydroelectric power station at Three Gorges Dam in China. It produces enough electricity to power an area the size of the Netherlands.

• **The largest solar power station** is Nevada Solar One in the Mojave Desert, USA. It covers an area of more than 162 hectares (400 acres).

• **A single bolt of lightning** contains 5 billion joules of energy. If you could find a way to harness that energy, it would power a house for more than a month.

• **Just 5 per cent of the energy** used by an incandescent light bulb is used to make light. The other 95 per cent produces heat. Energy-saving light bulbs are four times more efficient.

• **The world's strongest magnet** is an electromagnet made by the Florida State University. It is 500,000 times stronger than Earth's magnetic field.

Natural history facts

OLDEST LIFE

• **The oldest living thing** on Earth is the giant seagrass that grows in the Mediterranean Sea. Some of it may be 200,000 years old.

• **The longest-lived animal** is the clam, which can live for more than 400 years. Of animals that move around, the bowhead whale may be the longest lived – one whale was recorded to have lived for 211 years.

• **The oldest trees** on Earth are bristlecone pines, some of which are more than 5,000 years old.

• **The oldest group** of living things still around today are archaea (bacteria-like single-celled life forms). They evolved more than 3 billion years ago, soon after the very first life forms appeared on Earth.

• **The earliest animals** on Earth were sponges, which lived in the oceans more than 700 million years ago. The first land plants appeared 425 million years ago. Dinosaurs appeared 230 million years ago.

• Spores of **rod-shaped bacteria that are 250 million years old** have been brought back to life by scientists.

• **Humans** first evolved in Africa about 200,000 years ago. They left Africa to spread across the world about 90,000 years ago.

• **Dinosaurs** were once thought to have died out 66 million years ago. But scientists now think that birds are their direct descendants and should be thought of as living dinosaurs, so the dinosaurs really did not die out at all.

Scientists think there are about 8.7 million species of living thing on Earth. About 90 per cent of them have yet to be discovered!

BIG AND SMALL

• The **biggest animal** that has ever lived on Earth is the blue whale, a mammal that can grow up to 30 m (100 ft) and weigh 180 tonnes. Possibly the **smallest animal** is the tardigrade, or water bear. This invertebrate can be just 0.1 mm (0.005 in) long.

• The **biggest fish** is the whale shark, which can grow to 18 m (60 ft). The **smallest fish** is *Paedocypris progenetica*, which is just 7.9 mm (0.3 in) long.

• The **heaviest bird** is the ostrich, weighing up to 156 kg (345 lb), which is too heavy to fly. The **heaviest flying bird** is the great bustard, which weighs 21 kg (46 lb). The **lightest bird** is the bee hummingbird, which weighs just 2 g (0.1 oz).

• The **largest insect** in the world is the giant weta, which weighs 71 g (2.5 oz). The **smallest insect** is the parasitic wasp *Dicopomorpha echmepterygis*, which is less than 0.2 mm (0.01 in) long.

• The **largest spider** is the goliath birdeater tarantula, with a leg span of 30 cm (12 in). The **smallest spider** is *Patu marplesi*, measuring 0.43 mm (0.017 in) – the size of the full stop at the end of this sentence.

• The **largest reptile**, the Nile crocodile, grows up to 6 m (20 ft) long. The **smallest reptile**, a dwarf chameleon, is about 28 mm (1 in) long.

• The **biggest amphibian** is the Chinese giant salamander, which can grow up to 1.8 m (6 ft) long. The **smallest amphibian** is *Paedophryne amauensis*, a tiny frog from Papua, New Guinea. At 7 mm (0.27 in) long, it is also the world's smallest vertebrate.

• The **smallest mammal** is the hog-nosed bat, also called the bumblebee bat, which weighs just 2 g (0.1 oz).

EXTINCT GIANTS

• The **giant moa** was the tallest bird ever, standing 3.6 m (12 ft) tall. It lived in New Zealand, and became extinct about 500 years ago due to hunting by humans.

• The **South American short-faced bear**, which lived about 1 million years ago, weighed 1.5 tonnes and stood more than 3.4 m (11 ft) tall when standing on its hind legs. It was twice the size of a polar bear.

• The **steppe mammoth** stood 4 m (13 ft) tall. Its tusks could grow to more than 5 m (16 ft) long. It lived in Siberia 500,000 years ago.

• *Josephoartigasia monesi* was a giant rodent that lived in South America 2 million years ago. It was the size of a small car, measuring 3 m (10 ft) long and weighing about 1 tonne.

• *Argentinosaurus* was one of the largest dinosaurs, measuring 30 m (100 ft) from head to tail, and weighed more than 70 tonnes. It laid eggs the size of a football.

• *Meganeura* was a giant dragonfly-like insect that lived 300 million years ago. It had a wingspan of more than 60 cm (2 ft).

Glossary

Acceleration A change in an object's velocity, caused by a force acting on it.

Amplitude A measure of the height of an energy wave. Loud sounds are made of sound waves with a large amplitude.

Atmosphere A layer of gases that surrounds a planet such as Earth.

Atom The smallest particle of a chemical element.

Bacteria Tiny single-celled organisms, found all over Earth.

Carnivore An animal, such as a shark, lion, or crocodile, that eats only meat.

Cell The smallest unit of a life form. Organisms can be single-celled or multi-celled.

Circuit A continuous loop around which an electrical current can flow.

Compound A substance made from two or more elements.

Condense To change state from a gas into a liquid.

Conductor A substance that allows electricity to flow through it easily.

Current A flow of electricity.

Decomposition A change that takes place in dead bodies, in which complex substances break down into simpler chemicals.

DNA A special substance found in the cells of all living things. The DNA contains instructions that tell the cells how to behave.

Ecosystem A distinct region, such as a forest or an ocean, which contains living organisms.

Electromagnet A powerful magnet made using electricity.

Electron A particle that makes up part of an atom. An electron has a negative charge.

Element A pure substance, such as gold, hydrogen, or oxygen, that is made up of only one kind of atom. There are 118 different elements.

Environment The surroundings in which an organism lives, including other organisms, together with conditions such as temperature and light.

Evaporation The change in state of a substance from a liquid to a gas.

Evolution The process by which species change into other species over very long periods. Evolution is the way life developed on Earth.

Fertilization The process by which male and female parts of an animal or plant come together to reproduce.

Force A push or a pull that changes an object's shape or velocity.

Fossil fuel Fuel such as coal and oil that is made from the remains of living things.

Friction A force caused by rubbing one thing against another. Friction slows down movement and produces heat.

Fulcrum The point around which a lever rotates.

Fungus A kind of organism that feeds on the bodies of living or dead plants and animals.

Gas A state of matter in which molecules are spread out and moving rapidly. Most gases are invisible.

Gear A simple machine that moves a force from one place to another and changes the size of the force.

Germination The process by which a seed begins to grow into a new plant.

Gills Parts of a fish that absorb oxygen dissolved in the water.

Gravity A force that pulls all objects with mass towards each other.

Herbivore An animal, such as a cow, elephant, or deer, that eats only plants.

Hypothesis A theory about how things work. Scientists test their hypotheses by carrying out experiments.

Inclined plane A simple machine used to lift or lower heavy objects using less effort.

Infrared A form of invisible radiation given off as heat by objects.

Insulator A substance that does not allow electrical current or heat to pass through it easily.

Invertebrate An animal that does not have a backbone.

Ion An atom or molecule that contains an uneven number of protons and electrons. An ion either has positive or negative charge.

Lever A simple machine that makes a force or a movement larger. Levers can be used to move heavy objects.

Liquid A state of matter in which a substance has a fixed volume but no fixed shape.

Mass The amount of matter within an object.

Matter Any physical substance.

Metabolism The chemical process by which living things make the substances they need to grow and stay healthy.

Migration A journey made by animals from one place to another in search of food or in order to reproduce.

Molecule A group of atoms that have bonded together to make a new substance. Water is made of molecules containing hydrogen and oxygen.

Neutron A particle found in the nucleus of an atom. It does not have a charge.

Nucleus The centre of an atom, made of neutrons and protons. Also used to mean a part of a cell that contains most of the cell's DNA.

Nutrient A chemical that a plant or animal needs to stay healthy.

Omnivore An animal that eats both meat and plants.

Orbit The path of an object that follows another object. The Moon makes an orbit around Earth.

Organism An individual living thing, such as a plant or animal.

Parasite An organism that lives on another organism and harms it.

Particle A very small bit of matter, such as an atom, a molecule, or an electron.

Photosynthesis A process that takes place in the leaves of plants, which use the energy of the Sun to make sugars they need as food.

Plasma A state of matter similar to a gas and containing charged ions.

Precipitation Water that falls to Earth's surface from the atmosphere. It can be in the form of rain, hail, or snow.

Predator An animal that hunts other animals for food.

Prey An animal that is hunted by other animals for food.

Protist A simple form of single-celled life.

Proton A particle found in an atom's nucleus. A proton has a positive charge.

Pulley A simple machine used to increase pulling forces.

Radiation A form of energy that travels in the form of electromagnetic waves, such as light and X-rays.

Respiration A chemical process in which food is broken down to release its energy.

Satellite An object that orbits another object. The Moon is Earth's only natural satellite.

Seed The fertilized egg of a plant, usually surrounded by a store of food to help it grow.

Solid A state of matter in which the molecules are tightly packed together and cannot move freely.

Solution A liquid with another substance dissolved in it.

Species A group of organisms that are very similar and able to breed with one another.

Spore A fertilized cell made by fungi that grows into a new organism.

Static electricity A form of electricity in which electric charge builds up in one place.

Temperature A measure of how hot a substance is.

Ultraviolet A form of radiation found in sunlight. Humans cannot see ultraviolet, but some insects and birds can.

Velocity The speed and direction of movement of an object.

Vertebrate An animal that has a backbone.

Wedge A simple machine that is used to separate objects or to hold them in place.

Index

Acknowledgments

Dorling Kindersley would like to thank:
Monica Byles for proofreading; Helen Peters for
indexing; Deeksha Saikia, Jessica Cawthra, Kingshuk
Ghoshal, and Francesca Baines for editorial assistance;
Dhirendra Singh, Revati Anand, Chrissy Barnard,
Govind Mittal, and Philip Letsu for design assistance;
Saloni Singh for the jacket; Bimlesh Tiwary, Dheeraj
Singh, Jaypal Singh, Pawan Kumar, Balwant Singh,
and Rakesh Kumar for DTP assistance; Deepak Negi
for picture research assistance; and David Almond for
pre-production.

**The publisher would like to thank the following
for their kind permission to reproduce
their photographs:**

(Key: a-above; b-below/bottom; c-centre; f-far; l-left;
r-right; t-top)

2-3 Dreamstime.com: Olivier Le Queinec. 4 Corbis:
Matthias Kulka (br). 5 Dreamstime.com: Epstefanov (t).
Fotolia: tacna (br). 6 Corbis: Bettmann (clb). Dorling
Kindersley: University Museum of Archaeology and
Anthropology, Cambridge (crb, br). 7 Dreamstime.
com: Erzetic (tr); Georgios Kollidas (br). 8 Corbis:
Underwood & Underwood (ca). 9 Dreamstime.com:
Andreniclas (bc); Orseng (tr). Getty Images: P Barber /
Custom Medical Stock Photo (ft). 10 Dreamstime.com:
Radu Razvan Gheorghe. 11 Corbis: Auslöser (b).
Fotolia: Gennady Poznyakov (tl). 12-13 NASA. 14
Dreamstime.com: Jason Yoder. 16 Fotolia: guy (b).
18 Dreamstime.com: Dmitriy Pichugin (b). 19 Corbis:
Brandon Tabiolo / Design Pics (tr). 21 Dreamstime.
com: Dan Talson (crb). 22 Dreamstime.com: Vadim
Ponomarenko (bl). 23 Corbis: Christian Hacker /
beyond (br). 25 Dreamstime.com: Konstantin Kirillov
(bl). 27 © CERN: (b). 28-29 Science Photo Library:
Cern, P Loiez. 30 Dreamstime.com: Michael
Thompson (cr). 31 Dreamstime.com: MinervaStudio
(br); Leon Rafael (cla). 32 Alamy Images: sciencephotos
(bl). 33 Dreamstime.com: Ongood (b); Michal Janošek
(tr). 34 Corbis: Paul Hardy. 35 Dreamstime.com:
Jovani Carlo Gorospe (br). 36 Dreamstime.com:
Vladimir Mucibabic (cl). 37 Dreamstime.com: Natalia
Bratslavsky (bc); Serban Enache (tl). 39 SuperStock:
Stock Connection (b). 40 Alamy Images: Liam Grant
Photography (br). 42-43 Corbis: Tim Clayton. 46
Dreamstime.com: Onimaru56 (bl). Getty Images:
Boston Globe (cr). 47 Dreamstime.com: William Attard
Mccarthy (bc). Getty Images: Diane Collins and Jordan
Hollender / Photodisc (bl). 48 Alamy Images: David Hall.
49 Dreamstime.com: Yalcinsonat (cb). 50 Corbis:
Serdar Tibet (cl). 51 Dreamstime.com: Redbaron (bl).
Getty Images: Jeffrey Coolidge / Iconica (tr). 52
Dreamstime.com: Anna Ceglińska (cla). Getty Images:
altanbanedo / Flickr (b). 53 Dreamstime.com: Norman
Chan (cra); Yao Zhenyu (cla); Oxfordsquare (br). 55
NASA: ESA / NASA / SOHO (crb). Science Photo
Library: US Department Of Energy (bl). 56 Dreamstime.
com: Juemic (t). 57 Dreamstime.com: Chris Hamilton (br).
Getty Images: Image Source (t). 59 Dreamstime.com:
Yuriy Shirokov (br). 60-61 Corbis: NASA. 64 Corbis:
Imaginechina (b). 65 Dreamstime.com: Mikhail
Kokhanchikov (tr). NASA: (bl). 67 Science Photo
Library: David R Frazier (b). 68 Dreamstime.com:
Elinur (br); Carla F Castagno (cra). 69 Dreamstime.
com: Starblue (bl). Getty Images: Comstock Images
(bc); SMC Images / Photodisc (cra). NASA: (br). 70-71
NASA. 72 Getty Images: Will Salter / Lonely Planet
Images (b). 73 Dreamstime.com: Arne9001 (bl); Olga
Popova (crb). NASA: (br). 75 Dreamstime.com: Elwynn
(b). Getty Images: PhotoPlus Magazine / Future (tr).
77 Corbis: Visuals Unlimited (cra). Dreamstime.com:
Wellphotos (t). Getty Images: Mark Kostich / Vetta
(br). 78 Corbis: Scientifica / Visuals Unlimited (bl).
Dreamstime.com: Allazzotova (cr). 79 Dreamstime.
com: Evgenyatamanenko (b). Fotolia: Marek (cr).
80 Dreamstime.com: JoyKdesigns (tr); Bob Phillips
(b). 81 Dreamstime.com: Andrey Vergeles (c). 83
Dreamstime.com: Frenc (tr); Refocus (b). 84 NASA:
Scott Andrews / Canon (l). 85 Corbis: Peter Turnley (t).
86 Corbis: Martin Philbey (b). 86-87 Corbis: Philip
Wallick (t). 88 NASA: (t). 88-89 Dreamstime.com:
Terencefoto (b). 89 Dreamstime.com: Ivan Cholakov
(br); Nivi (tr). 90-91 Getty Images: Willoughby Owen /
Flickr. 92 Dreamstime.com: Jaroslaw Grudzinski (cr);
Jiri Hamhalter (tr). 93 Dreamstime.com: Falun1 (c). 94
Dreamstime.com: Leloft1911 (cr). Serg_velusceac (b).
95 Corbis: Glowimages (b). Dreamstime.com: 96
Science Photo Library: Maximilian Stock Ltd. 97
Dreamstime.com: Uatp1 (br). 98 Corbis: Bettmann
(cl). Dreamstime.com: Leung Cho Pan (bc). 98-99
Getty Images: AFP / Stringer (b). 99 Dreamstime.com:
Paul Hakimata (tr). 100 Dreamstime.com:
Tommy Schultz. 101 Corbis: Dr Thomas Deerinck /
Visuals Unlimited (bl); Andrey Sukhachev (crb). 103 Alamy
Images: Digital Archive Japan (b). 104 Corbis: Micro
Discovery (b). Dreamstime.com: Saša Prudkov (r).
104 Dreamstime.com: Ruud Morijn (cr). 106 Getty
Images: Wim van Egmond / Visuals Unlimited, Inc (cb).
106-107 Dreamstime.com: Monkey Business Images
(b). 107 Dreamstime.com: Evgeny Karandaev (tr). 108
Dreamstime.com. 108-109 Dreamstime.com: Alain
Lacroix (b). 109 Dreamstime.com: Martin Green (bc).
110 Dreamstime.com: Chuyu (b). 111 Dreamstime.
com: Hupeng (cr); Petitfrere (tl). 112-113 Corbis:
Steven Vidler / Eurasia Press. 115 Dreamstime.com:
Yaroslav Osadchyy (t). 116 Dorling Kindersley: Lucy
Claxton (tr). 117 Dreamstime.com: Alex Bramwell (c);
Richard Griffin (br). 118 Dreamstime.com: John Casey.
119 Dreamstime.com: Marietjie Opperman (ca);
Dariusz Szwangruber (cb); Nancy Tripp (br). 120-121
SuperStock: Juniors. 122 Dreamstime.com: Tdargon
(cr). 123 Dreamstime.com: Scot22 (br). 124 Corbis:
Stephen Dalton / Minden Pictures (t). 125 Corbis:
Fotofeeling / Westend61 (b). Dreamstime.com:

Steveheap (t). 126 Dreamstime.com: Spaceheater (c);
Sergey Uryadnikov (clb). 126-127 Dreamstime.com:
Tom Uhlman (b). 127 Corbis: Wim van Egmond /
Visuals Unlimited (b). Dreamstime.com: Dekanaryas
(c); Sergey Uryadnikov (tc). 128 Dreamstime.com:
Lilkar (b). 129 Dreamstime.com: Saskia Massink (br);
Orlando Florin Rosu (c). 130 Dreamstime.com: Most66
(cl); Nico Smit (c). 131 Corbis: Sergius Fomine / Global
Look (tr). Dreamstime.com: Anton Foltin (br); Kmitu
(clb); Irabel8 (bc); Hiroshi Tanaka (b). 132-133 Getty
Images: Jeff Hunter / Photographer's Choice. 134
Dreamstime.com: Jamiegodson. 135 Alamy Images:
Tom Uhlman (b). Corbis: Science Picture Co / Science
Faction (t). Dreamstime.com: Dejan Sarman (tr). 136
Dreamstime.com: Dongfan Wang (c). 137 Corbis:
Birgitte Wilms / Minden Pictures (cla). Dreamstime.
com: Serena Livingston (b). 138 Corbis: Michael
Durham / Minden Pictures (cla). 138-139 Dreamstime.
com: Gordon Miller (c). 139 Corbis: Joe McDonald (br).
Dorling Kindersley: Booth Museum of Natural History,
Brighton (c). 140 Dreamstime.com: Davepmorgan (l);
Vladimir Seliverstov (br). 141 Dorling Kindersley:
American Museum of Natural History (b). Getty
Images: De Agostini (t). 142-143 Dreamstime.com:
Pklimenko (b). 143 Corbis: Jeffrey L Rotman (br).
Dreamstime.com: Meryll (t).

Cover images: Front: Alamy Stock Photo:
Jupiterimages clb; Corbis: Mark Weiss ca; Dorling
Kindersley: Richard Leeney / Bergen County, NJ,
Law and Public Safety bl, Stephen Oliver fcla; Getty
Images: Oliver Cleve r; Spine: Getty Images: Oliver
Cleve

All other images © Dorling Kindersley

For further information see:
www.dkimages.com